Biography as High Adventure

Biography as High Adventure

Life-Writers Speak on Their Art

Edited with a Prologue by
Stephen B. Oates

The University of Massachusetts Press

Amherst

Copyright © 1986 by The University of Massachusetts Press
All rights reserved
Printed in the United States of America
Set in Linoterm Trump Medieval at The University of Massachusetts Press

Library of Congress Cataloging-in-Publication Data

Main entry under title:
Biography as high adventure.
Includes index.
1. Biography (as a literary form)—Addresses,
essays, lectures. I. Oates, Stephen B.
CT21.B468   1986   808'.06692   85-20847
ISBN 0-87023-513-3 (alk. paper)
ISBN 0-87023-514-1 (pbk. : alk. paper)

"Biography as a Work of Art" is reprinted from André Maurois's *Aspects of Biography*
© Nov. 19, 1956, by Appleton-Century-Crofts, Inc.
  "The Figure under the Carpet" is reprinted from *Telling Lives: The Biographer's Art*,
ed. Marc Pachter (1979); subsequently revised and published as "Myth" in *Writing Lives,
Principia Biographica*, by Leon Edel. Reprinted by permission of the author and the pub-
lisher, W. W. Norton & Company, Inc. Copyright © 1984, 1959 by Leon Edel.
  "Walking the Boundaries" is reprinted from *The Art of Biography* by Paul Murray
Kendall by permission of W. W. Norton & Company, Inc. and George Allen & Unwin.
Copyright © 1985 by Stephen B. Oates. Copyright © 1965 by W. W. Norton & Company, Inc.
  "Biography as Agent of Humanism" by Frank E. Vandiver was first presented at the
1982 Texas Lecture and Symposium on the Humanities, sponsored by the Texas Com-
mittee for the Humanities. From James F. Veninga, ed., *The Biographer's Gift: Life Histories and Humanism* (Texas A & M University Press, 1983).
  "The Biographer's Relationship with His Hero," from *Biography: The Craft and the
Calling* by Catherine Drinker Bowen, copyright © 1969 by Catherine Drinker Bowen, is
reprinted by permission of Little, Brown and Company and Harold Ober Associates,
Incorporated.
  "The Real Life" by Justin Kaplan was originally published in *Harvard English Studies*
8 (1978) © 1978 by the President and Fellows of Harvard College and is reprinted with
the author's permission.
  "The Burdens of Biography" by Mark Schorer was originally published in the *Michi-
gan Quarterly Review* (Autumn 1962) and is reprinted with permission of *Michigan
Quarterly Review*.
  "Biography as a Prism of History" by Barbara Tuchman was originally published in
Telling Lives: The Biographer's Art, ed. Marc Pachter (1979) and is reprinted with per-
mission of Russell & Volkening, Inc., as agents for the author. Copyright © 1979 by
Barbara Tuchman.
  "Reassembling the Dust" by Paul Mariani was originally published in the *New En-
gland Review* (Spring 1983).
  "Biography as High Adventure" by Stephen B. Oates was originally published in
Timeline (June–July 1985).

BOOKS ON DEMAND
This edition has been produced using digital technology that allows the publisher
to reprint small quantities "on demand."
The textual content is identical to that of previous printings,
but reproduction quality may vary from the original edition.
Printed by BookMobile.

To the memory of

Mari Sandoz

Whose *Crazy Horse* helped show the way

Contents

Prologue

Biography is currently enjoying immense popularity in the United States. The number of biographical titles published each year has virtually doubled since the 1960s, and for good reason. Biography may now be the preferred form of reading in America. A recent survey by the Library of Congress indicated that more people had read a biography in the previous six months than any other kind of book.

How to account for biography's appeal? For one thing, it personalizes events, demonstrates that the individual does count—which is reassuring to people in our complex, technical age, who often feel caught up in vast impersonal forces beyond their control. For another, "people are naturally curious about lives," says biographer Nancy Milford. "What we really want to know is, 'How do I live?' So to read about other people's lives is a sort of guide."

Biographer Jean Strouse offers another reason. "We read biography the way we used to read novels. For access to human experience: a life that has a beginning, a middle, and an end." Biographer W. Jackson Bate agrees. The current popularity of biography, he contends, is "the result of the decline of the old Victorian novel as a big, panoramic portrayal of a slice of life. In most novels since Thomas Mann, story and hero have been lost. The novel is no longer the prevailing form. Biography is stepping into the breach, portraying particular people and times the way the great novels of the past did."

Bate, of course, is talking about a particular kind of biography—the kind that employs fictional techniques without resorting to fiction itself. The life-writer who does this, as Desmond McCarthy says, "is an artist on oath." He cannot invent facts, but he can give them narrative form to tell a story. Paul Murray Kendall calls this "pure biography," whose mission is "to elicit, from the coldness of paper, the warmth of a life being lived."

This form of biography needs to be carefully distinguished from two other biographical approaches: the critical study and the scholarly chronicle. All, to be sure, are legitimate methods of writing about individuals—in fact, many biographies contain elements of all three approaches. Yet in their ideal form they have different purposes and techniques, and for clarity we need to understand what these are.

The critical biography, enormously popular in academe, is analogous to the formal lecture in which the author alone occupies the stage. At his literary podium, he analyzes his subject with appropriate detachment and skepticism, comparing his subject with similar lives in other eras, offering judgments about significance and consequence, often using psychoanalytical language to explain his character, perhaps dazzling the audience with his erudition and argumentative force. The action here is almost entirely intellectual; our minds are engaged, not our hearts; our focus is on the author, not the subject. The subject may be quoted to illustrate a point in the lecture, but he is never brought to life. That, of course, is not the author's purpose, for he is involved in critical discussion, not in art.

By contrast, the scholarly chronicle is a straightforward recitation of facts. The opening lines of Constantine Fitzgibbon's *Life of Dylan Thomas* are typical of the approach: "Dylan Marlais Thomas was born on the 27th of October, 1914, in his parents' house, No. 5 Cwmdonkin Drive, which lies in that part of Swansea called the Uplands. He was the only son and younger child of D. J. Thomas and of his wife Florence Hannah, nee Williams." The narrative voice is dry and detached, the prose informative—and utterly lifeless. We read the scholarly chronicle to gain information about its subject, not to be swept up in a powerful story.

A pure biography, on the other hand, attempts to narrate a life story. To paraphrase Kendall, it is the simulation of a person's life, based on all that is known about that person. If done well, pure biography is something that literate people of whatever station or profession can enjoy and benefit from. In pure life-writing, the biographer lets his subject have the whole stage, with just enough historical backdrop for us to understand the subject in proper context. Functioning as "the hidden author," to use Wayne Booth's term, the pure biographer makes his subject come alive through graphic scenes, telling quotations, apt details, character development, interpersonal relationships, intellectual and emotional struggle, and dramatic narrative sweep. To give a sense of a life unfolding, the pure biographer is careful to tell his story sequentially, never topically. "Thematic groupings," warns Kendall, "cannot be permitted to block or deform the sweep of chronology, the sequential heart-beat of a life, the 'faring onward' of our tragi-comic journey. They cannot be deployed like the topics of an expository essay—exposition is the enemy of biography, dead tissue cumbering a living organism."

The pure biographer is also careful not to lapse into critical commentary or psychoanalytical speculation. He must, of course, have psychological insights, for without them he could have no conception of character, no understanding of interpersonal relationships. But he shuns critical and psychological speculation because it destroys narrative. As biographer Justin Kaplan points out, "you can't write a narrative and after every paragraph or two come to a dead stop and say this is what I've done and this is what I've demonstrated. It really all comes down to the business of how to tell a story."

By telling a story, the pure biographer hopes to engage our hearts as well as our minds. As readers, we become active participants in the drama, as though we are with the subject as he lived his life. We identify with him and his relationships, with his ideas and feelings, his anxieties and joys. We are alternately enlightened and moved; we may even cry—out of compassion, or heartbreak, or exaltation. We are involved, too, because the biographer-artist does not try to explain everything, instead relying on the power of suggestion to let us reach our own conclusions, make our own discoveries, have our own "ah-hah!" experience. By story's end, we have come to know the subject so intimately that his death may leave us with a profound sense of loss. Certainly, we have learned a great deal about the times, for biography humanizes history; it helps us live through the times ourselves. But we have also witnessed another's long journey through the vicissitudes of life. We have seen how somebody in another age suffered personal dilemmas like our own—identity crises, ambivalences, hurts, setbacks, even a loss of will—which he anguished over and tried to work his way through. We have felt the subject's struggle, his failures, his triumphs and glories, as though they were our own. We close the book feeling uplifted, for our emotions and our minds have both been edified.

While Kendall calls this "pure biography," perhaps a more meaningful term would be *literary* biography. Most often the term is used to describe lives of literary figures. But, in the present volume, Justin Kaplan argues that "a strong case should be made for enlarging the term 'literary biography' to include books that have literary qualities and not necessarily literary subjects." The term would encompass biographies that attempt to create a life through the magic of language, that seek to illuminate universal truths about humankind through the sufferings and triumphs of a single human being.

It is understandable why this form of biography might appeal to a broad reading audience. There are those, of course, who argue that the "analytical mode" is the only way to truth, and who disparage pure biography as "superficial," "boring," even "anti-intellectual." Perhaps Virginia Woolf, a biographer in her own right, provides the best answer to that. "By telling us the true facts, by sifting the little from the big, and shaping the whole so that we perceive the outline, the biographer does more to stimulate the imagination than any poet or novelist save the greatest. For few poets and novelists are capable of that high degree of tension which gives us reality."

This volume is concerned exclusively with biography as a narrative art, comprising essays by ten people who have actually practiced the form. No academic theorists, these. I chose them because they are, or were, experienced biographers who spoke from firsthand knowledge when they addressed the nature, challenge, and hazards of biography. They not only explain in detail what life-writing is, but recount the burdens, the excitement and adventure, of the process itself. In addition, they afford rare insight into that unique interaction between two humanities that is the essence of life-writing. And they suggest what a versatile form it is, with Barbara W. Tuchman describing how biography among other things can serve as a window to an age.

Not that the contributors agree on all aspects of biography as narrative. For example, there is general disagreement as to how much of the subject's inner life can be known. All would acknowledge that the biographer must look for what André Maurois called "the hidden unity of a life," but they differ on what that means. For Leon Edel, it means finding "the figure under the carpet," that is, the psychological signs and evidence that reveal the subject's "hidden personal myth." Paul Mariani describes the discovery of that inner life as "the moment of the breakthrough"—"that moment of light streaming into the head, the moment of the rainbow." Frank Vandiver, on the other hand, contends that a biographer cannot know his subject's thoughts unless they are expressed somewhere. Justin Kaplan and Mark Schorer, for their part, discuss how difficult it is to get at the subject's real or inner life, which is why biography at best, as Kaplan puts it, "is only a plausible, inevitably idiosyncratic surmise and reconstruction, severely limited by historical materials that are loaded with duplicities and evasions."

There are differences, too, about the biographer's proper relationship with his subject. While Maurois and Tuchman call for detachment and distance, most of the others advocate compassion and empathy, even love. Several of the contributors divide over a particularly provocative question: should the life-writer show his subject's darker side, his bedwetting as a child, his obscenities in language, even his sexual behavior? Must the reader know about the subject's dark shadows in order to understand and appreciate his life?

Yet the contributors would agree on certain essentials: that the function of biography is to evoke and dramatize a life through novelistic techniques but not invention itself, and that it should emerge from painstaking research—"the first thing a biographer must be is a drudge"—and intimate familiarity with the places where the subject lived and died. All would agree that the writer of lives must be selective in his choice of details, must eschew psychological jargon and write "in the language of literature," must let the subject "have the whole floor" and "speak in his own words and stance," must present a portrait that is "dramatically and psychologically coherent" and that makes the subject live in a living world.

I hope that the essays add up to a fascinating portrait of biography as a form of art. To my knowledge, no other collection offers such varied and trenchant discussion about the craft by ten writers who have actually made the journey. Perhaps the volume will create the illusion of ten biographers sitting in a room together, sharing their thoughts and experiences with you as well as with one another. That they might disagree only underscores the challenge of trying to recreate "this magnificent poetry of life," as Maurois says, to capture its truths and its eternal mysteries.

Biography as High Adventure

One

Biography as a Work of Art

If we could place ourselves in the position of the artist for the contemplation of our own lives, those lives would certainly give us
intense aesthetic pleasure. No novelist or biographer can ever show
us such fine shades of feeling as those which we could distinguish if
we could contemplate our own loves, our own ambition, our own
jealousy, our own happiness. But at the moment at which we ourselves display emotion, we are incapable of observation. Our emotions are too strong and leave no faculty of aesthetic criticism at our
disposal. It might be easier, perhaps, to feel some aesthetic emotion
from the contemplation of the lives of those around us; but nearly
always we have a feeling either of affection or of antipathy toward
them, and here again the strength of such feelings robs us of an attitude of detachment.

Miss Jane Harrison in her *Ancient Art and Ritual* explains this
admirably:

> To see a thing, to feel a thing, as a work of art, we must, then,
> become for the time unpractical, must be loosed from the fear and
> flurry of actual living, must become spectators. Why is this? Why
> can we not live and look at once? The fact that we cannot is clear. If
> we watch a friend drowning we do not note the exquisite curve
> made by his body as he falls into the water, nor the play of the sun-
> light on the ripples as he disappears below the surface; we should
> be unhuman fiends if we did. And again, why? It would do our
> friend no harm that we should enjoy the curves and the sunlight,
> provided we also threw him a rope. But the simple fact is that we
> *cannot* look at the curves and the sunlight because our whole
> being is centered on acting, on saving him; we cannot even, at the
> moment, fully feel our own terror and impending loss.

How, then, is a human life to give us aesthetic pleasure? First, it
must be so lightly linked to our own, that, as we contemplate it, we

4   feel no need of doing anything, no moral impulse; and to that end, perhaps the best means is that we should know it to be unreal, as when we read a novel. If we were David Copperfield and had Dora for a wife, it would be a pathetic situation, of which we should not savor the beauty. In the novel, we contemplate it as a shipwreck in a picture, without feeling the need of swimming and of clutching at the nearest piece of vegetation. Certain novelists kill this aesthetic pleasure by forcing the reader to take part when they themselves set out to solve the ethical problems which their books present. But the best of them realize that this is not the artist's business. Chekov, for instance, wrote to his friend Suvorin: "You are confusing two things: the solution, and the correct statement, of a problem. The artist is concerned only with the second. In *Anna Karenina* no problem is solved, but the book is completely satisfying since all the problems are well stated."

But this is not the only reason why the novel appears to lighten the load of our own feelings and passions. The novel is a thing we can understand. In real life, living human beings are dangerous enigmas; it is impossible to foresee their actions; ideas seem to come to them, and then to fly away with confusing rapidity; amidst such disorder the intellect has great difficulty in finding its way. As we stand before our friends or our enemies, it is as though we stood watching a drama of infinite complexity of which we know not, of which we never shall know, the end. On the other hand, a character in a novel is built up of what the author has put into it; it is the creation of a human intellect and, as such, is accessible to a human intellect. We have no longer to deal with a divine and inexhaustible multiplicity but with a measurable and human simplicity. Of course the character may be complex (the creations of modern novelists nearly always are), but even this complexity is an ordered complexity and we can grasp it. Consider Mr. Forster's *A Passage to India:* his characters are very finely shaded. He has aimed at, and succeeded in, showing us the delicate differences between the European and the Asiatic ways of thinking. Nevertheless his book is quite clear—much more so than India itself, that mysterious country with its millions of souls in which we might travel for years without understanding it. What art is concerned with is a picture of reality sufficiently far removed from us to relieve us of the desire to do something, and at the same time directed by a human will. We come back to the old Baconian definition: *Ars est homo additus naturae.*

These two qualities, then, which are essential for all aesthetic activity—an ethical neutrality and a reconstruction of nature by man—are a source of some embarrassment to us today as we attempt to treat of biography considered as a work of art; for they appear to debar biography, as well as history, from admission to the domain of art. In the first place, the characters of a biography are not so well adapted as those of a novel to relieve us of the necessity of acting and judging, since they have actually existed. We feel no need of judging Anna Karenina or Becky Sharp, because the people who were made to suffer by them are themselves characters in a novel. But if we read a life of Byron, we feel that there really was an actual Lady Byron, an actual Lady Caroline Lamb, and our moral impulses are stirred at the expense of our aesthetic emotions. This applies even more strongly when a statesman is concerned. When an Englishman reads a life of Gladstone or of Peel, his political and historical passions are naturally aroused and rob him of the necessary detachment. But this objection, by no means a negligible one, applies with especial force to the life either of someone still living or of someone only recently dead. As soon as the hero is dead, and dead for a sufficiently long time to relieve the reader of any feeling that what he is reading may wound a widow or a child still living, a veil of peace and security spreads itself in a remarkable way over the finished picture. Death is the greatest of the artists; by his passing, all passions are set at rest.

Perhaps biography even has an advantage over the novel. When we read the biography of a very well-known man, we know in advance what changes of fortune and what *dénouement* to expect. At first sight we might think that this might rob the book of some of its interest; but if the thing is well done, the effect is exactly the reverse. When we go to see a tragedy we know perfectly well that Caesar will in the end be murdered by Brutus, we know perfectly well that Lear will go mad; but the slow march of the drama toward these events for which we are waiting endows our emotion with that poetic grandeur which the ever-present idea of Destiny gives to Greek tragedy.

In the same way, when we read a life with the events and the end of which we are already familiar, we seem to be walking in a stretch of country which we know already, and to be reviving and completing our recollections of it. The peace of mind with which we accomplish this familiar walk is favorable to the proper aesthetic attitude. Tragic beauty is, moreover, enhanced when there is a sad ending to the life. Mr. Laurence Housman tells the story of a conversation in which Oscar Wilde explained that a life, in order to be beautiful, must end in disaster, and quoted Napoleon as an example, showing that if

6   there had been no St. Helena, his life would have lost all its tragic value. One cannot help thinking that Wilde's own career owes most of its interest to the catastrophe which ended it. Sometimes the disaster is less obvious. In the case of Lord Beaconsfield the superficial observer gets an impression of marvelous success: all the ambitions of his boyhood were fulfilled in his old age. But there was an intellectual disaster, nevertheless. Measure the difference between the political vision of the Disraeli of the Young England period and the actual achievements of the aged prime minister and you will experience a feeling of the vanity of all things—not an ethical, but an aesthetic, feeling.

The fact, then, that the characters of a biography are real does not prevent them from being material for works of art. But there remains a second objection. We have said that the essential quality of a work of art is that it should be concerned with natural subjects reconstructed by the human spirit. *Ars est homo additus naturae.* It is essential that the spirit should have freedom of action. We know how a novelist constructs his characters: he builds them up out of feelings which act upon one another like the cogwheels of a well-made machine; if he is a novelist of genius, the machine is so well covered in flesh that it becomes almost invisible. But it still remains a machine and the most complex hero of a novel is infinitely less complex than the most simple of human beings.

It is not so easy to understand how it is possible to construct a historical character without spoiling him. He was what he was. We cannot change him. Think of Ruskin, think of Gladstone; they were real living beings like you and me, like our friends; each of them was to those who knew him a problem, confronted by which his friends passed their lives without being able to establish any order in an overabundant mass of observations and impressions.

What is the biographer to do? Must he try to re-create this living problem? The problem is made up of a vast accumulation of details and it would take a lifetime to get through them. Ought he to group the details as in a well-designed portrait? In that case he is getting away from the real thing.

"It appears to me," says Gilbert Mauge, "that in a life which is barely ended and still fresh in the memory there is an extraordinary folly which disappears as the years roll on and that biographers fall in with this process and construct those cold, finished systems to which they give the name of Henry II or Louis XII." To make of a man a system consistent with itself, clear, yet false, or to give up all attempts at making an intelligible system of him—such is the dilemma of the biographer.

The argument is a strong one, but it can prove equally well the impossibility of painting a landscape or a living face, since the face is too full of movement and the landscape has too much light and shade, too many different forms. Still, it is possible to paint a portrait or a landscape which may be at once a faithful image and a thing of beauty. The biographer, like the portrait painter and the landscape painter, must pick out the essential qualities in the whole subject which he is contemplating. By such a choice, if he can make the choice without weakening the whole, he is very precisely performing the artist's function.

The first choice he must make is that of a subject. A landscape painter does not set himself down anywhere. He stops before a natural landscape and says, "That is well placed, or well grouped." Some of the great impressionists used to walk about with a frame which they tried on various aspects of the landscape before choosing the subject for their painting. So too the biographer should walk about, frame in hand, and the choice of subject is perhaps the most important thing of all for him. There are lives which have a natural beauty, which, either by chance or by some force inherent in their being, are somehow constructed like spontaneous works of art. Sometimes they display that mysterious symmetry which, when concealed under an ample clothing of flesh, endows human works with beauty. Shelley's life, for example, is a wonderful natural composition; it is grouped round two women, Harriet and afterwards Mary Godwin. Each of these women corresponds with a different stage in Shelley's ethical development and he is drawn to each by feelings which bear a fairly close resemblance to each other. The catastrophe which ends his life occurs in early youth, before the point at which the crowded and varied events of a ripe age can rob his personality of its admirable simplicity. Byron is a much more difficult hero; a novelist would have been hard put to it to construct a life as fully charged with incident as that of Byron. Nevertheless his life must also have its hidden unity; the problem is to find it.

Sir Sidney Lee writes on this question of choice that the subject of a biography "should be of a certain magnitude." One might argue that the life of every human being is interesting and that, if a biographer were capable of analyzing all the thoughts which passed through the mind of an obscure beggar, such an analysis might have

8   greater richness and beauty than a life of Caesar. Sterling, to whom
     Carlyle devoted two volumes, was not a well-known character and
     Carlyle knew it. You remember his conclusion:

> All that remains, in palpable shape, of John Sterling's activities
> in this world, are those two poor volumes; scattered fragments
> gathered from the general waste of forgotten ephemera by the piety
> of a friend; an inconsiderable memorial, not pretending to have
> achieved greatness; only disclosing mournfully, to the more ob-
> servant, that a promise of greatness was there. Like other such
> lives, like all lives, this is a tragedy; high hopes, noble efforts;
> under thickening difficulties and impediments, ever-new noble-
> ness of valiant effort;—and the result death, with conquests by no
> means corresponding. A life which cannot challenge the world's
> attention; yet which does modestly solicit it, and perhaps on clear
> study will be found to reward it.

Marcel Schwob is of Carlyle's opinion:

> Biographers have supposed that only great men's lives could
> interest us. Art takes no account of such considerations. In the
> eyes of a painter the portrait of an unknown man by Cranach is
> worth as much as the portrait of Erasmus. The excellence of this
> latter picture is not due to the name of Erasmus. The biographer's
> art should contrive to set as great a price upon the life of a poor
> actor as upon the life of Shakespeare. It is a base instinct which
> makes us note with pleasure the shortened protuberance of the
> breast-bone in the bust of Alexander or the wisp of hair on Napo-
> leon's forehead. The smile of Mona Lisa, of whom we know noth-
> ing (perhaps it is a man's face), is more mysterious. A grimace
> drawn by Hokusaï leads to still deeper contemplation. If we were
> practicing the art in which Boswell and Aubrey excelled, we would
> certainly not have to describe minutely the greatest man of our age
> or to record the characteristics of the most famous men of the past,
> but to recount with the same care the individual lives of men,
> whether god-like, commonplace, or criminal.

A charming passage, but not wholly fair, I think. The characteristic feature of the life of an unknown man is that it leaves little
trace; unless one has in mind a man of genius who has written admirable letters and has not had them published. But then, by pub-
lishing them, we bring him into the category of great writers. The
novelist's choice is quite different from that of the historian. The

novelist is not bound by an oath to be strictly true and to make use of nothing but documents and authentic facts. Consequently, he is entitled to analyze an unknown and commonplace character, to make him speak and think. But what can the unfortunate biographer say of a man who has left no letters, no diary, no testimonies of friends, no sign of his actions? There is only one case in which this choice may be open to him—the life story of a character with whom he has lived. Certainly a Boswell could have "boswellized" an obscure friend of this kind, just as he boswellized Doctor Johnson, but it is extremely probable that the result would have been less interesting.

There is another argument in favor of the choice of men who have played an important part in history or in art and that is that the very expression "to play a part" is in this case something more than a metaphor. A man who exercises some lofty function (whether it be that of king or general or that special attitude which respect for his own genius imposes on a poet) reaches the point of literally "playing" a part; that is to say, his personality loses something of that obscure complexity common to all men and acquires a unity which is not wholly artificial. A great man—and often a king who is not a great man—finds himself modeled by the function he has to perform; unconsciously he aims at making his life a work of art, at becoming what the world would have him be; and so he acquires, not against his will, but in spite of himself and of whatever may be his intrinsic worth, that statuesque quality which makes him a fine model for the artist. Mr. Strachey, you may be sure, did not choose Queen Victoria by accident; if Queen Victoria had not been a queen, she might have been an interesting old lady to meet; but she would not have had in her that strange and subtle element of poetry which came to her by virtue of a combination of mediocrity as a woman with the fundamental quality of a queen.

Now let us assume that the subject is chosen. Can we suggest any rules which will enable the biographer to avoid making his subject dry, and, while maintaining a scrupulous respect for scientific truth, to get somewhere near the art of the novelist? Many historians think not; some have said "No" with severe emphasis. But a Lytton Strachey certainly believes it to be possible and, like Diogenes, gives practical proof of it. Let us try to discover a few of the rules.

The first, in my view, is that of consistently following a chronological order. The ancient biographers did not follow this plan. Plutarch begins by recounting the deeds of his heroes and, at the end of the life, collects those anecdotes which illustrate character. It is an odd method, since it deprives the reader throughout the story of the interest which an intimate knowledge of the hero would add to it. Plutarch's example was followed for a very long time and it is really a very remarkable instance of imitation; for there appears to be no other reason to explain why Doctor Johnson and many Victorian biographers collected at the end of a life what they call "personal traits of character." Even the *Dictionary of National Biography*, well constructed and remarkable as it is from other points of view, accepts, as an unchangeable rule, the order: facts first, character afterwards.

It seems to me extremely difficult to interest a reader in facts which are not presented in their normal order. The romantic interest of a life springs from just that anticipation of the future, from that finding of ourselves on the brink of the abyss which is Tomorrow, without any conception of what we shall find there. Even when the man is famous and the reader knows perfectly well that the hero is destined to become a great general or a great poet in the end, it seems rather absurd to tell him so in the first sentence of the book. Why begin a biography as Forster begins that of Dickens? "Charles Dickens, the most popular novelist of this country and one of the greatest humorists which England has produced, was born at Portsea on Friday, 7 February 1812."

No; no popular novelist or great humorist was ever born. There was born on 7 February 1812 a little baby, just as a little baby was born on Wellington's, or on Shakespeare's birthday.

Are we then to pretend ignorance of what we know perfectly well? Are we to pretend, at the beginning of a life of a great general, that we have forgotten the whole of his career? Strictly speaking, I think we are. It is an artifice, perhaps, but the word "artifice" contains the word "art." The author of a tragedy does not suggest to us, in his first few lines, what the *dénouement* is to be. The author of a biography realizes, of course, that the reader knows the *dénouement*; but it is not for him to advertise it on the first page. He must begin simply, with no desire to shine, but with the one object of placing his reader in an atmosphere which will facilitate his understanding of the first feelings of the hero in his youth.

Perhaps we may feel the need for chronological sequence more keenly than the old biographers because we do not believe, as they did, in the existence of unchangeable characters. We accept the evolution of the individual spirit just as we accept the evolution of the race. We believe that character develops but slowly, by contact with human beings and with events. A character always consistent with itself at every moment of the life of the hero is for us an intellectual abstraction; it is not a reality. Our point of view is that put by Miss Lowell at the beginning of her biography of Keats: "My object has been to make the reader feel as though he were living with Keats, subject to the same influences that surrounded him, moving in his circle, watching the advent of poems as from day to day they sprang into being."

It is difficult to make biography a work of art if the influence of events and people on the hero's character is not shown progressively and as they appeared to him. For instance, in a biography of Byron, it would not, in my view, be allowable to present a portrait of Shelley as he was before the moment when Byron first knew him, and it is desirable that the portrait should be as close as possible to what Shelley was in Byron's eyes at that moment.

One of the fundamental facts of life is the slow process of change in the minds of each one of us and in the characters of our friends. One whom we have regarded as perfect suddenly appears to us as fallible. This happened with Shelley and Godwin; it happened with John Manners and Disraeli. It is not the busness of the biographer to anticipate the discoveries of his hero. Nothing tends more to destroy the sense of movement than such a sentence as: "Though his impression had been favorable, he was afterwards to discover. . . ." Mr. Forster, following the French philosopher Alain, explained in his lectures on the novel that this question of the point of view is of the first importance in the construction of a novel. Three solutions are possible: either to see everything through the hero's eyes; or to see the action through the eyes of each one of the characters in turn; or to take the point of view of a creator and so make the action dominated by the novelist himself.

For biography I frankly prefer the first method, though I do not forget the necessity of occasionally taking up such a position at an infinite distance, in order to show how the hero is reflected in the faulty mirrors represented by the people who surround him.

In particular, great historical events bound up with the life of a statesman ought not to be treated in a biography as they are treated in a history. If a man is writing a life of Napoleon, his real subject is the spiritual and emotional development of Napoleon; history should be seen only in the background and to such a degree as may be necessary for the understanding of this development, and the biographer must try to give it something of the appearance which it had in the emperor's eyes. Take a simple instance like the battle of Austerlitz. In a well-written history it may, it ought, to be described in all its aspects; in a biography of Napoleon it should be the battle which Napoleon conceived and saw. A good example of this is the battle of Waterloo, as seen by Fabrice at the beginning of *La Chartreuse de Parme*.

Edmund Gosse has put the point very well:

> Broad views are entirely out of place in biography; and there is no greater literary mistake than to attempt what is called the *Life and Times* of a man. History deals with fragments of the vast roll of events; it must always begin abruptly and close in the middle of affairs; it must altogether deal, impartially, with a vast number of persons. Biography is a study sharply defined by two definite events: birth and death. It fills the canvas with one figure, and other characters, however great in themselves, must always be subsidiary to the central hero.

Another characteristic quality of a work of art is the choice of details. A scholar, as such, may accumulate an enormous number of facts on any subject and display them all without selection. But, I believe that, in fact, a great scholar makes his selection from the beginning and, by tracing certain general lines, produces an artist's work. The biographer who is also an artist must, above all things, relieve his reader of the burden of useless material. It is his duty to read everything himself, because, if he does not, he risks missing an important detail or accepting a fact as authentic which other documents prove to be false; but, once his scaffolding is firm and his house built, he pulls down the scaffolding and is at pains to present to the reader the completed house and nothing more.

Biography, in my view, does not consist in telling all one knows—for in that case the most trifling book would be as long as life itself—but in taking stock of one's knowledge and of choosing what is essential. It goes without saying that in making this choice, the biographer often finds himself tempted to emphasize that particular aspect of a character which he knows and loves best. From this it sometimes comes about that the hero is distorted by the artist-biographer. But is less distortion wrought by the bad arrangement of documents, by the absence of "values" (in the painter's sense), in the work of the heavy-handed biographer who produces a dull portrait of a striking countenance?

In this discarding of the useless, the biographer must not lose sight
of the fact that the smallest details are often the most interesting.
Everything that can give us an idea of what the man actually looked
like, the tone of his voice, the style of his conversation, is essential.
The part played by the body in helping to form our ideas of the character of our acquaintances should always be borne in mind. For us
a man primarily consists of a certain physical aspect, a certain look,
familiar gestures, a voice, a smile, a series of habitual expressions; all
these must be made to live again for us in the man who is presented
through the medium of a book. It is the historian's most difficult
task. The personality transmitted through documents is above all
things an abstract personality, hardly known except by his actions
toward his fellowmen. If he is not capable of making us see a being of
flesh and blood behind the clouds of papers and speeches and actions,
he is lost.

Marcel Schwob says,

> Historical science leaves us in uncertainty about individual
> people. It merely shows us their points of contact with general
> events. It tells us that Napoleon was ill on the day of Waterloo,
> that we must attribute Newton's immense intellectual activity to
> the absolute continence of his personal temperament, that
> Alexander was drunk when he killed Clitus and that Louis XIV's
> ulcer may have been the cause of certain of his decisions. Pascal
> argues about Cleopatra's nose—what would have happened if it
> had been shorter?—and about the grain of sand in Cromwell's
> bladder. All these individual facts matter only because they have
> modified events or because they might have altered the order of
> events. They are actual, or potential, causes. They must be left to
> scholars.
>
> Art is the exact opposite of general ideas. It describes only what
> is individual and desires only what is unique. It does not classify;
> it takes things out of their classes. So far as we are concerned, our
> general ideas may be like those which obtain in the planet Mars,
> and three lines which cut each other must make a triangle in any
> part of the universe. But consider a leaf of a tree, with its wayward
> system of colors varying with sun and shade, the swelling pro-
> duced on it by a single raindrop, the tiny hole made by an insect,
> the silvery track of a little snail, the first fatal gilding which is the
> sign of autumn; try to find a leaf exactly like it in all the great
> forests of the earth; I defy you to find it. There is no science of the

14   teguments of a leaflet, of the filaments of a cell, of the curvature of
a vein, of the violence of a habit, of the idiosyncrasies of a character. That a man had a twisted nose, or one eye higher than the
other, or knotty arm-joints; that he was accustomed to eat a *blanc
de poulet* at a particular hour, that he preferred Malvoisie to
Château Margaux—these are things without parallel in the world.
Thales might have said, "Gnothi seauton" just as well as Socrates,
but he would not have rubbed his leg in prison in the same way
before drinking the hemlock. Great men's ideas are the common
heritage of humanity; their only individual possessions are their
oddities. The book which should describe a man in all his incon-
sistencies would be a work of art like a Japanese print, displaying
a series of pictures of a tiny caterpillar seen once at one particular
hour of the day.

The strength of Aubrey and of Boswell lies exactly in their gusto
for such details. Boswell has given us a perfect idea of what Johnson's
tone of voice may have been. Marcel Schwob rejoices in the fact that
Diogenes Laertius

informs us that Aristotle carried on his stomach a leather purse
full of warm oil and that after his death a number of earthenware
jars were found in his house. We shall never know what Aristotle
did with all these bits of pottery; and the mystery is as delightful as
the mystery in which Boswell leaves us in the matter of the use
Johnson made of the dried orange-peel which he was in the habit of
keeping in his pockets.

Aubrey tells us that Spenser was a little man, that he wore his hair
short with a little collar and cuffs; that Erasmus disliked fish and
that none of Bacon's servants dared appear before him without boots
of Spanish leather, "for he would smell the neates-leather, which of-
fended him." It is impossible to understand the 18th Brumaire unless one knows that on that day Napoleon had pimples and had
scratched himself—hence his gory face and the mistake of the
grenadiers.

There is nothing more delightful in the writing of a biography than
the pursuit of vivid details like these across the pages of memoirs and
letters. Sometimes one may read hundreds of pages without finding
anything but general ideas—and those false ideas. Then, quite suddenly, in the byway of a phrase there appears a sign of life and the
faithful reader stops and grasps it. What a joy, for instance, to dis-

cover that d'Orsay used to laugh loudly when he said "Ha, ha," and gripped his friends' hands too vigorously. Mr. Strachey plays this game admirably: he knows that the little Victoria used, in her childhood, to be taught by the Baroness de Späth to make little cardboard boxes trimmed with gold paper and painted flowers. He notes that Victoria's journal has the appearance of being written by a child, but that her letters seem to be the work of a child corrected by a governess. He brings before our eyes an evening party at Windsor—the circle of people at the round table, the albums of the queen's sketches, with the prince playing his interminable games of chess with three of his gentlemen-in-waiting. No one was ever more conscious of the importance of authentic detail than the hero of the best of all biographies, Doctor Johnson himself:

> The business of a biographer is often to pass slightly over those performances and incidents which produce vulgar greatness, to lead the thoughts into domestick privacies, and display the minute details of daily life, where exterior appendages are cast aside, and men excel each other only by prudence and by virtue. . . .
>
> There are many invisible circumstances which . . . are more important than publick occurrences. Thus Sallust, the great master of nature, has not forgot, in his account of Cataline, to remark that *his walk was now quick, and again slow*, as an indication of a mind revolving something with violent commotion.
>
> Thus the story of Melanchthon affords a striking lecture on the value of time, by informing us, that when he made an appointment, he expected not only the hour, but the minute to be fixed, that the day might not run out in the idleness of suspense: and all the plans and enterprizes of De Witt are now of less importance to the world, than that part of his personal character, which represents him as *careful of his health, and negligent of his life*.
>
> But biography has often been allotted to writers who seem very little acquainted with the nature of their task. . . . They rarely afford any other account than might be collected from publick papers, but imagine themselves writing a life when they exhibit a chronological series of actions or preferments; and so little regard the manners or behaviour of their heroes, that more knowledge may be gained of a man's real character, by a short conversation with one of his servants, than from a formal and studied narrative, begun with his pedigree, and ended with his funeral.

16   From this passage it is clear that Johnson had a vision of what a certain type of biography might be, the type which was later to be exemplified by Mr. Strachey. Moreover, as one reads Johnson's own *Lives of the Poets,* one is struck by the Stracheyesque touch to be found in many of them. In fact, one has but to entitle one half of the work *Eminent Jacobeans* and the other *Eminent Augustans* to make it a wholly modern book. Milton undergoes at Johnson's hands a much severer treatment than Cardinal Manning at Mr. Strachey's: "Milton soon determined to repudiate her for disobedience; and, being one of those who could easily find arguments to justify inclination, published (in 1644) *The Doctrine and Discipline of Divorce.*" Johnson is full of touches of this kind.

Must I confess that, as a work of art, I prefer *Eminent Victorians*? Johnson's moral judgments crop up with a vigor which is entertaining but at the same time spoils, or at least displaces, the effect. "The brutality of his invective," he says again of Milton, "was equaled only by the vulgarity of his flattery." This is, in my view, a form of judgment too heavy to be delivered by the biographer on the subject of a biography. Objectivity and detachment are the supreme aesthetic virtues. Like the novelist, the biographer must "expose" and not "impose." A great life well told always carries a suggestion of a philosophy of life, but it gains nothing by an expression of that philosophy.

Can a biography have a poetic value? I think it can. Poetry, in the wide sense, I conceive to be a transmutation of nature into some beautiful form, made intelligible by the introduction of rhythm. In poetry, in the stricter sense, this rhythm is established by the verse form or by rhyme; in music, by the motif; in a book by the recurrence, at more or less distant intervals, of the essential motifs of the work.

A human life is always made up of a number of such motifs; when you study one of them, it will soon begin to impress itself upon you with a remarkable force. In Shelley's life the water motif dominates the whole symphony. It is by the banks of a river that we first find him dreaming in his youth at Eton; it is on a stream that he afterwards launches his fragile and symbolical paper boats; then his life is spent in ships; his first wife, Harriet, dies of drowning and the vision of a watery death haunts the reader for a long time before the actual event, as though Destiny had been leading Shelley from childhood toward the bay of Spezzia.

In Disraeli's life there is a flower motif, which sometimes takes the form of a pot of geraniums sent by his sister, sometimes of the queen's primroses; there is an Eastern motif, clear and piercing, which sounds with a blare of trumpets in youth, but gradually the brazen sounds are softened and, as death approaches, are nothing but a distant echo muffled by the strains of English violins; and there is the antagonistic rain motif, that terrible English rain which sets out to extinguish the over-brilliant Eastern flame and succeeds; the rain which at the beginning puts to flight the muddy knights of the Eglinton tournament, the rain which submerges Peel and robs the Hughenden peacocks of their feathers; the rain which in the end carries off the sun-kissed wizard himself.

Of this magnificent poetry of life Mr. Strachey has made himself a master, and I know few finer passages than those last pages of *Queen Victoria*, in which he shows us all the motifs of the queen's life passing through her dying consciousness:

> The spring woods at Osborne, so full of primroses for Lord Beaconsfield . . . Lord Palmerston's queer clothes and high demeanor, and Albert's face under the green lamp, and Albert's first stag at Balmoral, and Albert in his blue and silver uniform, and the Baron coming in through a doorway, and Lord M. dreaming at Windsor with the rooks cawing in the elm trees, and the Archbishop of Canterbury on his knees in the dawn, and the old king's turkey-cock ejaculations, and Uncle Leopold's soft voice at Claremont, and Lehzen with the globes, and her mother's feathers sweeping down towards her, and a great old repeater-watch of her father's in its tortoise-shell case, and a yellow rug, and some friendly flounces of sprigged muslin, and the trees and the grass at Kensington.

It is a page that makes one think of the funeral march of Siegfried, or of the motifs of the Tetralogy as they return shrouded in crêpe at the end of the *Twilight of the Gods*. The mind savors a poetic melancholy at this rapid survey of the past. We gather up in one poor bunch the rare blooms which have given a life its perfume, and we offer them to the Fates which have been fulfilled. It is the last refrain of a dying song, the last stanza of a consummated poem. Here the biographer is on a level with the great musician and the great poet.

Two
Leon Edel

The Figure under the Carpet

A portrait gallery—a national portrait gallery—evokes great pages of history, the distant and the near past. It is an exhilarating experience to come upon faces of characters one has known only in history books. I remember a particular thrill of my youth when I wandered into the rooms of Britain's National Portrait Gallery housing the eminent Victorians—so eminent, so assured, so rubicund, so gouty, so marked in feature and countenance. At that moment I crossed a magical threshold of the past. I was at large in the nineteenth century with Spencer and Huxley, Darwin and Green, Gladstone and Disraeli. Equally thrilling was the experience of finding myself among writers all the way back to the Romantics—Byron, sexy and sultry in his Eastern turban; Shelley, looking startled; Coleridge, broad and large as life; the Brontës on a primitive canvas painted by their brother, the canvas by which we alone know them. There is a fascinating relationship between the painter or sculptor who, with his plastic resources, gives us the visual appearance of a life and a personality, and the biographer who traces these features in an essay or book. It is fairly obvious that a painted portrait or a chiseled bust cannot be a total biography. But at its best, when the bust or the portrait comes from the hand of a master, it is certainly more than a mask, it is an essence of a life, usually a great life, and it captures—when painterly eyes and shaping hands have looked and seized it—certain individual traits and features and preserves them for posterity, for that life beyond life, of which Milton so eloquently spoke. Biography seeks to arrive at similar essences. I speak inevitably of the large figures, of endowed renderings. We need not concern ourselves with "camp" biographies or daubs, the ephemeral figures of movie stars, dope addicts, Boston stranglers; they belong to certain kinds of life histories written by journalists in our time. They belong in a wax works. They are documentary and often vividly mythic; they are more related to the photographic, the visual

interesting parallel

capturing life

moment, the changing world of entertainment or crime, the great and flourishing field of interminable gossip disseminated by the media. This is quite distinct, as we know, from serious artistic biographical and pictorial quests to capture the depths and mysteries of singular greatness. *Forms of biography*

There are painted portraits then that are mere facades; there are biographies that are mere compendiums. Thomas Sergeant Perry, an early American critic, long ago described the latter. "The biographer," he wrote, "gets a dustcart into which he shovels diaries, reminiscences, old letters, until the cart is full. Then he dumps the load in front of your door. That is Vol. I. Then he goes forth again on the same errand. And there is Vol. II. Out of this rubbish the reader constructs a biography." A compendium is like a family album: a series of pictures, selections from an archive. The biographer producing such a work often pretends that he is allowing the character to speak for himself or herself. This is an ingenuous way of avoiding biographical responsibility. That responsibility involves not only accumulating and offering facts: it entails the ability to interpret these facts in the light of all that the biographer has learned about his subject. The general public, reading biographies with delight, seems unaware of how they originate. And criticism seems to me to be wholly negligent in not informing them. I know of no critics in modern times (and in an age that has given itself more to criticism than to creation) who have chosen to deal with biography as one deals with poetry or the novel. The critics fall into the easy trap of writing pieces about the life that was lived, when their business is to discuss how the life was told. Perhaps this is because biography seems to them a mix of too many things—like the opera. It involves reportage, research, interrogation of witnesses, village or urban gossip, staged events, arranged scenes, the laws of evidence, massed documents and archives, kinescopes, tape recordings, and who knows, maybe computers as well, in addition to photographs and statues with broken noses. Yet out of this material the marvelous can emerge—the story of a given life. And when such a story is read, the readers forget that it has been fashioned out of facts and words. They seem to think, like Walter Cronkite, that this is the way it is—when this is not at all the way it is: for everything is seen through particular eyes, like the painter's portrait. "How," exclaimed Virginia Woolf when she sat down to write the life of the critic and artist Roger Fry, "how can one make a life of six cardboard boxes full of tailors' bills, love letters and old picture postcards?"

endless resources

20   How indeed! This is perhaps our little secret, and it baffles the critics. The biographer, after all, is as much of a storyteller as the novelist or historian; indeed, he is a specialized kind of historian. And we have only to read Virginia Woolf's biography of Roger Fry to discover how she brilliantly shifted from the art that imagines its facts to the art that imagines the form into which facts must be put. In summary, condensation, and vivid pictorial effect I consider Mrs. Woolf's *Roger Fry* one of the most beautiful biographical portraits of our time. Here, for example, is the beginning of her chapter on the post-Impressionists:

puts you there with them

> To a stranger meeting him then for the first time (1910) he looked much older than his age. He was only forty-four, but he gave the impression of a man with a great weight of experience behind him. He looked worn and seasoned, ascetic yet tough. And there was his reputation, of course, to confuse a first impression—his reputation as a lecturer and as an art critic. . . . He talked that spring in a room looking out over the trees of a London square, in a deep voice like a harmonious growl. . . . Behind his glasses, beneath bushy black eyebrows, he had very luminous eyes with a curious power of observation in them as if, while he talked, he looked, and considered what he saw. Half-consciously he would stretch out a hand and begin to alter the flowers in a vase, or pick up a bit of china, turn it round and put it down again.

power of words

I have presented enough here to suggest to you how, in the hands of an artist, the word can be used to paint a portrait. In one hundred words Virginia Woolf paints a picture, ready to be hung, of Roger Fry at forty-four. In these few sentences she has told us a great deal not only about his appearance, his eyes, his physical being, but also his character, the restlessness of it, the energy of his fingers reaching out, touching the shape of things, composing, arranging.

I have often said that a biographer is a storyteller who may not invent his facts but who is allowed to imagine his form. He is like the sculptor who doesn't invent his clay, or the painter who doesn't invent the tubes out of which he squeezes his paint. The biographical imagination is exercised upon gathered data; and the squeezed colors may not be mixed or blended. They can only be arranged. Biography is the art of human portrayal in words, and it is a noble and adventurous art. There are many ways of making portraits. We know how a painter can give voices to an entire wall; and how a sculptor with skill of eye and chisel brings durable life to marble. So a biographer

Art of biographies

about the subject, not the author

fashions a man or a woman out of the seemingly intractable materials of archives, diaries, documents, dreams, a glimpse, a series of memories. The biographer who respects his craft makes his figure speak in its own voice and stance. I think this is what Lytton Strachey had in mind when he said that the biographical art was "the most delicate and humane of all the branches of the art of writing." I'm not sure that it's more humane than poetry or the novel, but it touches us just as intimately, for it tries to tell a human truth, it stands for the thousands of things and people that the portrait gallery stands for. Yeats suggested that "we may come to think that nothing exists but a stream of souls, that all knowledge is biography"—and I gladly assent to this beautiful way of seeing life because all knowledge is mixed up with what goes on in human minds and in the senses that inform our body and give shape to our being.

Why?

Biography from time to time seems to have a frightening effect on creative artists. George Eliot called it "a disease of English literature." Vladimir Nabokov described it as "psycho-plagiarism." Auden repeatedly—even while reviewing biographies with delight for the *New Yorker*—called it "always superfluous" and "usually in bad taste." Unlike Yeats, unlike Henry James who called biography "one of the great observed adventures of mankind," these artists seem to be discussing certain kinds of biography that deal in the small coin of life, not the larger treasures—and they are worried about invasion of privacy. T. S. Eliot certainly was when he ordered that no biography be sanctioned by his heirs. Thackeray had done the same earlier, as did Matthew Arnold. Eliot put the matter clearly when he said "curiosity about the private life of a public man may be of three kinds: the useful, the harmless and the impertinent." And he claimed that the line "between curiosity which is legitimate and that which is merely harmless, and between that which is merely harmless and that which is vulgarly impertinent" can never be drawn precisely. I mention these opinions to show how widely apart men of genius are in their view of life portraits. We must regard what they say about biography as individual statements reflecting personal misgivings; they do not alter the fact of biography itself; they relate rather to how it is practiced. And now I can hear you ask why I call biography a young art, when we can summon Plutarch out of olden times and Boswell out of modernity. I see these men, centuries apart, as having laid certain cornerstones in the way in which Defoe laid a cornerstone for the novel by writing *Robinson Crusoe*. Plu-

9 "materials"

tarch shored up for us what remained of the great legends and myths of the noble Greeks and Romans. He assembled his materials—ancient lore, old wives' tales, stories of splendors and glories, miseries and defeats—traveling the length of the Mediterranean in his historical quest. We pay homage to him as a historian who sought the meanings of great lives as a form of moral philosophy. And Shakespeare paid biography his homage when he infused into Plutarch the divine poetry by which we today know his Roman plays—Caesar, Brutus, Mark Antony, and the others. Moving to the eighteenth century, we pay homage to Boswell for creating a unique work: that of staying close to his subject for a quarter of a century and writing minutes of the great man's talk that have the ring of truth. Biography rarely possesses conversation, and Boswell gave to his life of Dr. Johnson the valuable re-creation of the doctor's voice and his mind within that voice. In this sense he predicted the tape recorder and oral history—but tapes are mechanical records, unfiltered through a recording mind. Boswell, like Plutarch, is a foundation stone, not a model. Modern Boswells have ended in disaster. I have dreamed of writing an essay on them—how Robert Frost's Boswell began his work in love and adulation and ended in disparagement and hate; how Faulkner's listened to his talk of liquor and horses only to be frustrated by the writer's widow and some personal hindrance that so far he has not overcome; how Thornton Wilder named a young Boswell whose enthusiasm led Wilder to hastily withdraw; not to speak of Shaw's Boswell who wrote a fat book that bears unmistakable evidence that Shaw did much of the writing.

The great problem that we must face at the start is the oppressive weight of modern archives. Gone are the days when biographies could be written out of half a dozen shoe boxes, or pieced together out of little facts like the royal grant of wine to Chaucer, or Shakespeare's second-best bed. Fancy writing a biography out of a man's check stubs. From not having enough material, biography has come into the dubious possession of great wealth and more than it can absorb and digest. The modern archive preserves everything; entire libraries have been created for each of our recent presidents. Can a biographer afford to spend his lifetime wading through such great masses of paper, Himalayas of photographs, microfilms, kinescopes, and still emerge, if not suffocated, with any sense of a face or a personality? What comes out of these archives are books too heavy and too long. Did Lytton Strachey, that master of brevity, who put Queen Victoria into 300 pages out of *her* archives, which cover almost a cen-

↓ *easy to get lost in too much material/info*

tury, deserve almost a thousand pages for himself? Does Rex Stout, splendid detective-story writer though he is, need 600? or Gertrude Vanderbilt Whitney? Some sense of proportion is needed. I can hear you asking me, does Henry James deserve five volumes? I won't try to answer that question now but will confine myself to saying I believe this biography to be one of the shorter biographies of our time. I admire the British when they are able to tell us in 200 pages all we need to know of certain quiet lives. We do not need—as so many biographers seem to think—a record of every last date in a subject's datebook, a catalog of gourmet dinners, and chapter and verse on every glorious drunk, when these have such simple and familiar ritualistic beginnings—and archetypal endings. Nor do we need clouds of witnesses for every life—as exemplified in the lives of the two Cranes, Stephen and Hart, which occupy 800 pages of print each, even though the subjects died at thirty. To paraphrase Ruskin, it is not pleasant to have great parts of archives flung in a reader's face; and the subject ends up fenced in by walls of quotation and abysses of anecdote. Biography still has to learn the art of the portrait. It is all too often the work of journeymen, as Lytton Strachey said. Critics, poets, novelists, should write biographies. John Berryman performed a service when he wrote a life of Stephen Crane. Virginia Woolf was doing the same when she wrote her book on Roger Fry. And Norman Mailer, whatever his motivations, revealed a proper sense of biography when as a novelist he sought to capture a figure as elusive and as delicate as Marilyn Monroe. Even if we judge his work a failure, we must praise his undertaking. ↗ lack personality

[I do not disparage archives.] I simply groan when I see one. Those great cluttered masses of papers, those mountains of photographs in Texas of Lyndon B., and no doubt those endless tapes that will speak to posterity, like the recorded telephone calls of Treasury Secretary Henry Morgenthau. Who is to say what should be kept and what shouldn't? I remember finding a fur neckpiece in a box that contained letters of Henry James in the Library of Congress. The fur, I was told, was public property, and it was a question whether it should be quietly burned or properly sequestered. It told me merely that the lady who had received the letters got her archive mixed with her wardrobe. Yet perhaps that mangy little fur had its place. The oddest scrap of paper sometimes takes on an awesome significance after the passage of time, and I agree with T. S. Eliot that one never knows what a laundry list will reveal. No, we must allow papers to

↓ sometimes its the unsuspecting material

focus on the importance (handwritten annotation)

accumulate in a laissez-faire spirit, we must allow biographical subjects to fill entire barns with their Internal Revenue records and
political figures to gather the memorabilia so gratifying to their egos.
Our concern is how to deal with this clutter, how to confront our
subject, how to achieve the clean mastery of the portrait painter un-
concerned with archives, who reads only the lines in the face, the
settled mouth, the color of the cheeks, the brush strokes and pencil
marks of time. More often than not this offers us the revealing mask
of life. The biographer must learn to know the mask—and in doing
this he will have won half the battle. The other half is his real battle,
the most difficult part of his task—his search for what I call the
figure under the carpet, the evidence in the reverse of the tapestry,
the life-myth of a given mask. In an archive, we wade simply and
securely through paper and photocopies and related concrete materials. But in our quest for the life-myth we tread on dangerous speculative and inferential ground, ground that requires all of our attention,
all of our accumulated resources. For we must read certain psychological signs that enable us to understand what people are really saying behind the faces they put on, behind the utterances they allow
themselves to make before the world. The aggressive emotion that
masquerades as a cutting witticism; the excessive endearment that
conceals a certain animus; the pleasant joking remark that is ac-
companied by a hostile gesture; the hostile gesture that turns into
a pat on the back; the sudden slip of the tongue that says the opposite
of what has been intended. This is the "psychological evidence" a
biographer must learn to read, even as he learns to read the hand-
writing of his personality and his slips of the pen. Armed with this
kind of eyesight, a biographer reads much more in the materials than
any sketchers of facades. To my vision, Pope John Paul I expressed
a great deal when he refused to be crowned and asked for a simplifica-
tion of a ceremony old in history. By that one gesture, he told the
world the course of his apostolate, brief though it was. There was
a message in that decision—a message about power—which the ob-
servant might have read. And if I were writing the pope's biography,
I would start by seeking an answer to this important question.

The method I am proposing for biography is related to the methods
of Sherlock Holmes and also to those of Sigmund Freud. If one approaches an archive with the right questions, one carries a series of
important keys to locked doors. The right doors will open if the right
questions are asked; the mountains of trivia will melt away, and essences will emerge. Many historians have unconsciously worked in

this way, but I am not aware that we have consciously sought to describe a *method*. This is not easy, nor can this method be mechanically learned. It requires a certain kind of talent, a certain kind of inwardness to look at the reverse of a tapestry, to know when and where to seek the figure under the carpet. special skill

What do I mean by the hidden personal myth? Let me take a writer like Ernest Hemingway, whose life and habits have been widely recorded, not least by a circle of his relatives and friends. We know he liked to shoot, to fish, to drink; we know that he was boastful. He wanted to be champion. He wanted to fight wars—on his own terms—and shoot big game and catch the biggest fish and live the manliest life—the super-manly life. Was not one of his books entitled *Men Without Women*? That tells us something—though it may not be what you think. Small wonder that Max Eastman asked a very proper biographical question—why did Hemingway make such a fuss about the hair on his chest? And we remember that when Hemingway ran into Eastman in Maxwell Perkins's office at Scribner's, he proved Eastman's insight by demanding a fight. The two writers ended on the floor with a great flailing of arms and legs. "I wasn't going to box with him," Eastman said when he described the incident to me. "I just put my arms around him and embraced him." Hemingway wanted to prove he had hair on his chest. Now the obvious myth—and I choose Hemingway because he can be read so easily—was the novelist's drive to do the biggest, kill the biggest, achieve the greatest, and that is written large in all his books. A code of drive and courage, simple, direct, masculine, excessively masculine; and a code in the art of trying to shape and simplify and crystallize and not get too close to feeling. That is the manifest myth. But as a biographer, I go beyond this and ask—what does Hemingway express? What is Hemingway saying to us in all his books and all his actions? A great deal, and as is nearly always the case, much that is exactly the opposite of what he seems to be saying. A manly man doesn't need to prove his masculinity every moment of the day. Only someone who is troubled and not at all secure with himself and with his role puts up his fists and spoils for a fight over a casual remark by an easygoing and affectionate person like Max Eastman. The biographical questions multiply, and in effect we ask ourselves: What is Hemingway defending himself against, so compulsive is his drive toward action and away from examined feeling, so consistent is his quest to surpass himself, as if he always must prove—even after he has had the world's acclaim—that he is the best and the greatest.

Critics have remarked on this, and I say nothing that has not already been widely discussed—but it illustrates what I mean by the figure under the carpet. Hemingway's figure *in* the carpet is his pattern of seeking out violence wherever he can find it, seeking out courage, resignation, heroism, and perseverance, and avoiding too much feeling. But the reverse of the tapestry tells us that somewhere within resides a troubled, uncertain, insecure figure, who works terribly hard to give himself eternal assurance. Where there seems to be immense fulfillment, we discern extraordinary inadequacy—and self-flagellation and a high competitiveness; also, a singular want of generosity toward his fellow artists, since he must always proclaim himself the champ. Life reduced to the terms of the bullring and the prize fight is a very narrow kind of life indeed. The biography of Hemingway that captures the real portrait, the portrait within, still needs to be written. And what is important in Hemingway's archive, which is large, are the answers to the questions that will relate his doubts, his failures, his struggles, and not the answers to his successes that are written in the public prints.

I will now take an example less obvious and less well known—that of Henry David Thoreau. The biographers of Thoreau have always accepted his view of himself and his mission at Walden Pond "to suck the marrow of life," that is, to meditate and learn the virtues of simplicity and solitude, and not be a slave to the bondages of life, like mortgages and banks and the humdrum entanglements of the farmer for whom Thoreau expresses considerable contempt. *Walden* is a beautiful book, an exquisite distillation of the intentions and desires of Thoreau, a work of the imagination that pretends it is a true story, and it embodies a myth that all America—indeed the whole world— has adopted: that of getting away from the slavery of civilization, facing the world as God made it, not as man ravaged it. This is one part of Thoreau's story, and it is a part of his greatness. The question a biographer seeking the truth must equally ask if he wants to see the figure under Thoreau's carpet is, what motivated him to this idealistic undertaking? Why did he decide to build a hut? In other words, why—beyond his own beautiful rationalizations—did he *really* go to Walden Pond? That seems to be a difficult question to answer. Yet by focusing on it within the materials of Thoreau's life a number of answers emerge. There is that day the remarkable woodsman went fishing and in cooking the fish set fire to the woods and almost burned Concord down. There is the simple fact that the farmers had quite as much contempt for Thoreau as he had for them. There is the evidence that Concord thought him a man of enormous talent who idled his time away walking in the woods. There is the man who said he'd rather shake the outstretched branch of a tree than the hand of Henry Thoreau. And there is Emerson who quoted this over Thoreau's grave. Thoreau's hut, we learn, did not stand in great loneliness; he did not plant it in a wilderness. He planted it on Emerson's land on the shores of Walden with Emerson's consent. This made it easy for him to criticize those who had to pay rent or mortgages. The railway lay within easy distance. His mother's house was one mile down the road and, said the Boston hostess, Annie Fields, in her diary, David Thoreau was a *very* good son, "even when living in his retirement at Walden Pond, he would come home every day." Others have told us that he raided the family cookie jar while describing how he subsisted on the beans he grew in his field. To discover this, and to remember how often Thoreau dined with the Emersons, and gregariously joined the citizens of Concord around the cracker barrel in the local store, is to overlook his life struggle, the inner biographical problem that the literary portrait painter must face. The evidence can be read in the moving parable within the pages of *Walden*, which tells us more than a thousand letters might in an archive. Thoreau wrote: "I long ago lost a hound, a bay horse, and a turtle dove, and am still on their trail. Many are the travellers I have spoken concerning them, describing their tracks and what calls they answer to. I have met one or two who had heard the hound, and the tramp of the horse, and even seen the dove disappear behind a cloud, and they seemed as anxious to recover them as if they had lost them themselves."

Loss and anxiety about loss—a bay horse, a hound, a turtle dove. Thoreau's little parable, which he launches enigmatically in *Walden*, contains a great deal that a biographer needs to guide him into the reverse of the tapestry of the author of *Walden*. Here, in capsule, are the three members of the animal kingdom closest to mankind: the faithful hound, guide, protector, loving and lovable; the horse of Thoreau's time, plower of fields, the embodiment of strength, trust, and support, and the spirited symbol of all that is instinctual in man; and finally the turtle dove, the soft cooing swift messenger, bearer of tidings as in the Bible, symbol of love and of the Holy Ghost. The biographer of Thoreau must write not the story of a solitude-loving, nature-loving, eternally questing self-satisfied isolator who despises his neighbors, and is despised by them, but the story of a man who feels he has lost the deepest parts of him-

biographers to find the deeper meaning

28   self—without guide and support, without strength and love, a lost little boy of Concord, a loner, a New England Narcissus. The biography would have to be written not in a debunking spirit but in compassion and with the realization that this man who felt he had lost so much was able to transcend his losses and create an American myth and the work of art known as *Walden*.

Art of biography

Biography stated in these terms begins to become more than a recital of facts, more than a description of an individual's minute doings, more than a study of achievement, when we allow ourselves to glimpse the myths within and behind the individual, the inner myth we all create in order to live, the myth that tells us we have some being, some selfhood, some goal, something to strive for beyond the fulfillments of food or sex or creature comforts. I remember a young man who set out to write the life of Rex Stout, the creator of Nero Wolfe. He asked me how to go about his job. I found rising within me, out of unconscious dictation, the sentence: "You will have to find out why Rex, a king, sought to disguise himself as Nero, an emperor—and a bad emperor at that!" Those of us who still remember Rex Stout might have thought he had kingly ambitions, for he founded Freedom House, he fought for copyright, he became head of countless enlightened organizations. And he wrote a series of books in which a very benign fat man with an evil name, living in isolation, solves crimes and punishes miscreants and makes the good prevail. Indeed he hires a legman whose name is Goodwin—a winner of good. Do not laugh when I play with the nomenclature of biographical subjects: the names by which we are called, the names we call ourselves, these too are part of our myth. Rex Stout was a thin man and he made Nero Wolfe very stout indeed, 260 pounds, thus reversing the saying that in every stout man a thin man struggles to be freed. But if he had imperial dreams, why such a bad emperor? One can discover easily where the Wolfe comes from. Rex Stout's middle name was Todhunter—which is Scots for a fox hunter. So we see the series of metamorphoses, king-emperor, fox-wolf, thin-stout. An earlier detective created by Stout was named Tecumseh Fox—and this demonstrates how consistent the imagination of myth can be: Tecumseh was a very imperial Shawnee. Such literary games are amusing enough; they become more fascinating, however, when examined in the light of psychology. We learn in our inquiries that Rex Stout, in creating opposites of himself, was also consciously creating opposites of Sherlock Holmes, who was, as it happened, a tall thin man like Stout himself. He once told an inquirer he had decided that

Arthur Conan Doyle was the king of detective-story writers (how inescapable the designation "king") and, since he wanted the same kind of kingship, he decided to make Nero Wolfe the opposite in every way to Sherlock Holmes. Holmes played the violin, Wolfe raised orchids; Holmes took cocaine, Wolfe drank beer; Holmes went anywhere to solve a crime, Wolfe stayed at home.

This tells us that Rex Stout was engaged in a double process—that of creating a persona involving himself and an opposite to Doyle's detective with whom he was identified. He did something else. He followed Doyle in creating an American Dr. Watson who is Watson's opposite too—Archie Goodwin is as bright and keen as Watson is genially dull and phlegmatic. If we go back to look at Stout and Doyle themselves we discover that both were living out in their imaginations a king-myth or an emperor-myth. What fun it was for Doyle, a hard-working Victorian doctor turned author, to cut loose in his imagination and become Sherlock Holmes, to visit in fancy iniquitous dens, take drugs, and play a moody fiddle, while also retaining the bluff phlegmatic Victorian, Dr. Watson. What is this duality of the common self and the fantasy self but the creative and imaginative man tied to the usual and the routine and the bondage of society, seeking to escape by putting his literal and prosaic self into a persona—Dr. Watson or Archie Goodwin? On the other hand the imaginative self achieves freedoms beyond common reach, including victories over Scotland Yard or Manhattan police inspectors. I suspect that Doyle got most of his fun in life out of being Sherlock Holmes. But I discern, without going deeply into the matter, more trouble than fun for Rex Stout, who somehow had to choose the name of evil, that of a bad emperor rather than a good one, who turned foxes into wolves, because he perhaps was a bit afraid of his imperial dreams, and had some guilt about them. That need not concern us here. Let us leave the solution to future biographers. I think I have sufficiently shown the way in which we often play games of secret sharer—Joseph Conrad's term—with our mythic selves. The creative artist ends by turning his fantasies and problems into works that bring the fame and power that is sought—even as political figures through their acts create their public personae, even as our generals on occasion become their myths on the battlefield. In writing the lives of such men we find ourselves involved in a truly great adventure, and not merely that of archaeological digging among their archives, which any well-instructed graduate student can do. We go beyond this necessary routine into the search for an individual's hid-

"adventure"
↓ not just archives

30   den dreams of himself, and then discover how they have been acted out, either in an elaborate and imaginative defense against guilts and anxieties, as in Hemingway or Thoreau, or in a series of fantasy conversions or metamorphoses, as in Stout and Doyle. The biographer who writes the life of his subject's self-concept passes through a facade into the inner house of life.

We must recognize and not resist the modern explorations of the unconscious, the marvelous id-being with which we are endowed and where so many mysterious parts of life are enacted. This has opened up great new provinces for biographical knowledge and biographical exploration. What I enunciate is, I believe, a new principle for biography that has only just been adumbrated—that the writings and utterances and acts of any subject contain many more secrets of character and personality than we have hitherto allowed. A secret myth, as well as a manifest myth, as I say, is hidden within every creative life, and, in the gestures of a politician, the strategies of a general, the canvases and statues of art, and the life-styles of charismatic characters, we may discover more than biography has ever discovered in the past. Whole case histories can be compiled out of revealed experience—but we must compile them in the language of literature, not the language of therapy. We understand much more now about behavior and motivation. We understand much more how the rational mind, in concert with our senses, indulges in fantasies and sometimes translates these into realities. There are so many new ways, then, for drawing larger conclusions about an inner life, of which the outer life is a constant expression. Some such principles come to us from the new psychology.

new look at biographies

The National Portrait Gallery in London recently held a fascinating exhibition. They carefully gathered a series of portraits painted by the moderns—those who no longer paint faces simply as they see them. It was an exhibition that showed how cubists, vorticists, impressionists, and the other innovators of our time sought to put on canvas living subjects created out of new visions of reality. I would have difficulty describing in words the many rich things these portrait painters did—but it will best illustrate my point if I say to you that in Roland Penrose's portrait of his wife, he depicted in his surrealism birds and butterflies clustering along the mouth and eyes. And we know how revolutionary is Picasso's portrait of Gertrude Stein. I cannot remember when I found an exhibition more exhilarat-

new ways

ing. For what I saw was that these modern painters and sculptors— Picasso and Giacometti, Kokoschka and Matisse, Modigliani and Tchelitchev, and the earlier Gaudier-Brzeska—had all done exactly what I am saying the biographer must now do: they sought to go behind the facade, to penetrate the mask. There was Wyndham Lewis's Edith Sitwell, in which that lady was reduced to her flat-voiced impassivity, or Sickert's portrait of Edward VIII that caught in a strange and remarkable way that poor monarch's low self-esteem. Giacometti said of his sculptured portraits, "The adventure, the great adventure, is to see something unknown appear each day in the same face," and Picasso, speaking of his Gertrude Stein, said, "Everybody thinks she is not at all like her portrait but never mind, in the end she will manage to look just like it." Notable in the exhibition was Dali's portrait of Isabel Styles in which he managed to convey both external aspect and inner fantasy.

It was Graham Sutherland who best stated the case for biography in this exhibition. "I think it is true," he said, "that only those totally without physical vanity, educated in painting, or with exceptionally good manners, can disguise their feelings of shock or even revulsion when they are confronted for the first time with a reasonable truthful image of themselves."

For me these modern painters had with consistency carried the truths of their art into their representation of living persons as they had of landscape and rooms and the things that surround us in our world. They sought the inwardness and the myth; they did what Van Gogh did when he painted a chair or a picture of himself. They moved from the splendid verisimilitude of Rembrandt's self-portraits to a kind of Ur-portrait. In the re-creation of lives, we have reached a time when we must, like these painters, give a new account of ourselves. We must not flinch from the realities we have discovered; we must realize that beyond the flesh and the legend there is an inner sense of self, an inner man or woman, who shapes and expresses, alters and clothes, the personality that is our subject and our art. Archives become then simply illustrative—and by the method of seeking the secret self, the inner myth, our subjects stand revealed—not in the papers they accumulated but the works they wrought, the acts they performed, the shape they gave to their existence.

Three

Walking the Boundaries

Consider how uneasily biography lies between historical writing and belles lettres, somewhat disdainfully claimed by both.

For centuries, history regarded biography as a sort of poor relation, a hanger-on. An eighteenth-century historian perfectly reproduces the atmosphere of condescension when he confesses that he had "several times deviated and descended from the dignity of an historian, and voluntarily fallen into the lower class of biographers, annalists, etc." History regarded biography as trivial or, in kinder moments, fragmentary. The historian surveys the great scene. He deals with church and state, with the mighty issues of war and peace, with the growth of constitutions and the fall of kingdoms. The biographer contents himself with a single individual and the slight thread of happenings that form his life. *contrast*

In our own time this attitude has been, if not abolished, at least modified. Historians in increasing numbers—particularly since the Second World War—have themselves become biographers. Yet, fledgling historians in our graduate schools are not encouraged, I believe, to con biographies or study the methods of biographical research.

The distinguished American historian Dumas Malone, in an essay, "Biography and History," warns the biographer that "in his efforts to procure factual materials" he "must be as laborious and painstaking as any historian and he must be equally honest in interpreting them." Biography, then, if akin to history, had better wash its grubby hands before joining the company.

The essential nature of life-writing, however, becomes obscured if it is classed as a branch of history. Both explore the remains of yesterday and, as arts, interpret those remains; and there ends the similarity. Socrates and Cleopatra made their way in the world by their wits rather than by their beauty, but we should hardly class them as fellow intellectuals. The historian frames a cosmos of happenings, in which men are included only as event producers or event sufferers. The biographer explores the cosmos of a single being. History deals in generalizations about a time, the Middle Ages; about a group of people in time, the United States since 1865; about an institution, the Inns of Court in the fifteenth century. Biography deals in the particularities of one life.

The relations of biography with the art of literature have been almost as uneasy as those of biography with history. With this difference. Biography is a genuine province of literature—the notion is accepted by default rather than by debate—but a province which that kingdom has generally tended to ignore.

Our formal institutions of learning have paid scant attention to life-writing. In the United States the ubiquitous "survey courses" in English and American literature will yield a few pages of Pepys, a passage of Colley Cibber's autobiography, a little more from Johnson's *Lives of the Poets*, a prudently ample selection from Boswell's *Johnson*, something from Franklin's autobiography, a bit of John Stuart Mill and Cardinal Newman and Henry Adams, and—to balance the autobiographies—a chapter from Strachey's *Queen Victoria*. This, from *Widsith* to *Wasteland*, is about all.

American universities offer courses in "creative writing," nonfiction writing, even the writing of criticism; and graduate schools of English teach the mystique of the scholarly article. But universities do not offer courses in how to write biography, and few of them offer courses in the history and appreciation of biographical literature.

Until the twentieth century, scholars and critics found little to say about life-writing. In our own day biographical criticism has achieved notable stature, but it has been mostly written by a handful of biographers—Harold Nicolson, André Maurois, James Clifford, Leon Edel, Catherine Drinker Bowen, Mark Schorer, Iris Origo, and a few others. The massive annual bibliography of writings on English and American literature, which has been appearing in the Publications of the Modern Language Association (PMLA) since 1956, contains in its multi-thousands of listings over this period only four books and two considerable articles on biography. Historians of literature likewise take little interest in life-writing, as may be seen in two examples from Oxbridge. C. S. Lewis's much admired *English Literature in the Sixteenth Century* (Oxford) allows fewer than four pages to the three greatest biographical works of the age: More's *History of Richard III*, which inaugurates modern English prose, Roper's *Life of More*, and Cavendish's *Life of Wolsey*. The second

34   edition of *The Concise Cambridge History of English Literature* (1961) adds a chapter on "The Age of T. S. Eliot," which manages to mention political orators, writers on education, radio-television scripts, but has nothing to say about biographers—except to class Lytton Strachey as a caricaturist.

Perhaps scholars and critics feel, not that biography wants charm but that it wants challenge, that it does not need the services of an interpreter. Gourmets all, feeding on those "jellies soother than the creamy curd," which emerge from the kitchens of "imaginative literature," they can hardly be expected to burn with a hard gemlike flame if they are fired by mere meat and potatoes. Yet if we grant that a man's life is elusive, complex, subtly nuanced, it seems rather paradoxical to assume that the attempt to recapture that life is an enterprise too bald to repay investigation.

By and large, our best biographies present men of high action or men of letters. It is not hard to see why. The events in such men's lives—counting books, of course, as events—work like giant screens on which may be viewed the motions of personality. The cannons at Marengo hammer out, for that moment, Napoleon's character, as *Utopia*, more delicately, traces the psychic lineaments of Thomas More.

The greatest biography in the world unfolds the life of a man of letters; and literary figures have, in general, probably enjoyed a disproportionate amount of attention. For one thing, biographers, being writers of a kind, are attracted to writers, partly, no doubt, in order to seek their own features in a kindred face. Furthermore, men of letters are schooled, by temperament and talent, to examine themselves rather more assiduously than other beings do, and thus offer the biographer eloquent source-materials; and tend to project themselves by gesture as well as by pen, and thus provide the biographer with provocative role-playings against which he can stage his own perception of character.

On the other hand, the biographer of a man of letters runs special risks, the dangers lurking in the subject's words: there have probably been composed more disappointing lives of literary men than of any other kind of human being. In some cases, the works have been cavalierly ignored, or scanted; in others, they are too recklessly or crudely plundered as biographical evidences; in still others, they are mechanically shunted to one side and dealt with separately, as though the life and the "letters" did not penetrate each other.

The novels of the novelist, the poems of the poet, are significant events of a literary life, as the fighting of an election campaign, or a battle, are significant events of a life of action. Both are inextricably woven into the texture of living, and both harbor symbolic enactions of personality. But a poem-event is, paradoxically, more difficult to translate into biographical terms than an action-event. Whereas the poem is tantalizingly closer to the heart of self than such outward, limited manifestations of character as an election campaign, and appears to offer more direct expression of personality, it may well turn out to be a subtle concealment or a deliberately stylized projection or a privately visioned myth of that personality. A poem-event speaks a psychological language not always easy to understand but universal; poems and plays often whisper in a secret tongue—or light flares along a rocky coast to lure biographers to destruction.

Whatever paper trail the biographer treads, he shares the trials of other men of letters. The obvious difference between biography and poetry-novel-drama is, if enormous, not quite so enormous as appears. It will not do simply to say that biography is made out of fact (whatever that is) and fiction is made out of fancy (whatever *that* is). The writer of fiction, out of the mating of his own experience and his imagination, creates a world, to which he attempts to give the illusion of reality. The biographer, out of the mating of an extrinsic experience, imperfectly recorded, and his imagination, recreates a world, to which he attempts to give something of the reality of illusion. We demand that a novel, however romantic or "experimental," be in some way *true to life*; we demand of biography that it be *true to a life*. There is a difference in meaning between the phrases; they join, however, in signifying not "factual" but "authentic"—and authenticity lies not only in what we are given but in what we are persuaded to accept.

The biographer often finds himself in the grip of an extrarational, even compulsive choice, not unlike that which descends on the novelist or poet. The biographer's subject, it might be said, is a man whom he would have longed to create if he had not existed. Like the novelist, he must be continually asking questions about his materials and suspecting the form into which they, too quickly, fall—hoping for the patience to reject easy devices and plausible solutions and brilliant breakthroughs, so that he may trap those shy, belated birds, the best answers. The failed biography and the failed novel frequently suffer from an identical ill: the authors have taken their materials for granted.

36   In his questioning, the biographer, cherishing the obligations of
science and the hopes of art, teeters on a precarious perch. There are
times when he must resist the enticements of art in order to be true
to biographical art, must build with stone instead of rainbow. A literary device, however admirable in itself, which thrusts biographical
materials outside the dimensions of life-writing, ruptures truth
more seriously, because less obviously, than outright error. There
are times when the biographer must query apparent facts, "scientific" evidence, in order to be true to biographical science; must
build with rainbow instead of stone. Facts which mock his vision of
character may turn out not to be facts or to be facts which do not say
what they seem to say.

Since such struggles are hidden in the biographer's workshop, I
shall offer brief illustrations out of my own experience, both drawn
from a biography of that fifteenth-century political adventurer,
Warwick the kingmaker. His life spiraled to a culmination of violence and death in the battle of Barnet, which he fought against
Edward IV on Easter Sunday of 1471. The contemporary accounts of
the field are not numerous but offer more details than such reports
usually do.

Seeking to make as much as I could out of this last scene, both exciting and revealing, I cast the chapter in the historical present tense
in order to transport the reader into the thick of the action at Warwick's side. The chapter turned out bold and vivid, so I thought. But
my wife firmly informed me that it would not do, it did not ring
right. Grudgingly, I began asking myself questions, and soon received unpalatable answers.

In the first place, the historical present, a tricky device at best, gave
an unmistakably fictional air to the scene. What was worse, it
wrenched awry the style of the book. I do not mean simply the shift
from past tense to present. In biographical writing, one of the tasks
of style is to set the "viewing distance" between the reader and the
life. The distance should reflect the kind of materials out of which
the biography is created: the more intimate the evidence—letters,
diary, reminiscences—the nearer the reader can be brought to the
subject. Scantily documented Charlemagne and intimately observed
Winston Churchill refuse to dwell in the same biographical house.

No portrait of Warwick survives, no collection of family letters, no
view of him in undress. Hints of personality must be mined from
chronicle and document; his character displays itself on the large
screen of action. I had to reject the historical present because it

violated the "middle distance" already established, pretending to bring the reader closer to Warwick than the material warranted. If it seems obvious that I should have thought of all this before writing the chapter, I can but heartily agree.

In the second instance, an apparently documented fact collided head-on with my conception of Warwick himself and of his friend Louis XI of France, the famous "spider King." English accounts state that Warwick was paid for two journeys to the Continent in the summer of 1464. However, though he and Louis XI had indeed arranged a rendezvous for that summer, there is no record, or even the faintest suggestion, that the two met; and Louis's movements at this time were closely reported by the Burgundian historian Chastellain and by a Milanese ambassador who was a confidant of the king. Historians therefore assumed that Warwick had hidden himself at Calais, perhaps at the bidding of his sovereign Edward IV, who had no love for Louis.

This assumption, in my view, was false alike to the character of Warwick, who regarded himself as the mentor rather than the minister of King Edward, and to the character of King Louis, who was far too nervously voluble to have concealed an interview with the man of all men he longed to ensnare in his web and far too well informed to remain in ignorance of Warwick's presence at Calais. One document, a very solid-seeming document, was forcing the two men to behave as if they had fallen into trauma and lost their identities. The truth of fact simply did not square with psychological truth, as I saw it. Since I could neither accept nor ignore the former, I could only desperately scrabble for evidences to undermine it.

Fortunately, I at last dug out a series of counterfacts which indicated that Warwick was besieging castles in northern England at the time he was supposedly crossing the Channel, that the diplomatic journeys ascribed to him were actually made by two of his adherents, whose presence at Louis's court was fully vouched for, and hence that the clerk of the royal accounts, paying Warwick for his men's expenses, had wrongly assumed that the earl himself performed the service. In this case, pigheaded refusal to let "art" bow to "science" enabled me—I hope—to reconcile fact and vision, stone and rainbow.

There is one respect, quite apart from the practice of literary art itself, in which biography differs from purely imaginative literature.

The relations between the public and poetry-novel-drama are fre-

38   quently centered in the writer; whereas the relations between the public and biography are governed by subject matter. True, there are anthologies of poetry, drama, stories, arranged according to theme; and occasionally, no doubt, we decide to read love poetry or death poetry or an expressionistic play or short fiction dealing with suburbia. But more often we choose by author. We feel in a mood for Keats or Eugene O'Neill or Dickens, or we want to have another look at the Elizabethan sonneteers or at the ardent angularities of John Donne.

But we do not very often come to biography by thinking to ourselves: I want to read some Ludwig or some Maurois or some Marquis James. Rather, we desire to read a life of Napoleon or a life of Byron or a life of Andrew Jackson, or at least we choose according to categories of subjects: we have a hankering for medieval kings or nineteenth-century tycoons or Latin American adventurers.

The biographer does not regret this state of affairs; it is, indeed, the crown of his labors. The object of art, Horace reminds us, is to conceal art. The highest biographical art is the concealment of the biographer. Even Boswell illustrates this, for though he sometimes occupies space on the scene, he does so only to focus attention upon Johnson.

The other literary artists are unmistakably interfused in their work, identified with it. Despite stiff frowns from the new critics, we enjoy linking art with the artist. But we do not enjoy being aware of the biographer. Quite the contrary: being aware of the biographer spoils our illusion of sharing in a life. Unlike the poet, the biographer must have a talent for invisibility. Who would read "Ode to a Nightingale" in order to learn about nightingales? Who would read a life of Napoleon for any other reason but to know Napoleon?

Current definitions of life-writing are lucid and simple, but not altogether satisfactory. In *The Development of English Biography*, Sir Harold Nicolson seeks for the essence of biography in classifying the motives which lead to its creation. Thus he excludes biographies written in order to celebrate the dead, didactic biography, like the lives of saints, and all biographies written for some special end or from some special viewpoint. He concludes that "pure" biography comes into being when the author, eschewing all extraneous purposes, writes a life for its own sake, and, though adhering to truth, attempts to compose that life as a work of art.

In excluding the lives of saints or campaign biographies or pious memorials, Nicolson effectively clears the ground and takes us toward the heart of the matter. But can it be said that even the "purest" biographer is not moved by the commemorative urge? that he harbors, even if unconsciously, no didactic impulse? The barbaric yawp of an Assyrian king—his deeds and massacres preserved in stone—and the pawky Victorian eulogy are alike false to biography. But the fundamental emotion that powers biographical practice is surely the desire to mark, to keep alive, the passage of an individual by recapturing that life; what signals the pure biographer is that he regards the truth about a life as the only valid commemoration. Similarly, though the serious biographer eschews *overt* didacticism, it seems likely that he sweats over a life, say, of Henry James, not only because he regards James's life as suitable material for his art but also because that life, for him, says something or symbolizes something about the meaning of life in general that the writer is impelled to set forth.

Nicolson quotes approvingly the Oxford Dictionary's definition of biography—"The history of the lives of individual men as a branch of literature." In *The Nature of Biography*, John A. Garraty likewise defines biography as "the history of a human life" or "the record of a life." He explains, "It is thus a branch of history, each life a small segment in a vast mosaic. . . ." But biography, as we have seen, is not a branch of history; for history is not a mosaic of lives, that is, a vast accumulation of biographical sketches, but a generalized narrative concerning events, movements, institutions. Thus the phrase "history of a life," is confused and misleading. The alternate definition offered by Garraty, "the record of a life," is not much more satisfactory. For record implies documentation, severely factual account, an objective marshaling of evidences, and no biography which hopes to recapture the sense of life being lived, to suggest the mysteries of personality, can be any of these things.

Biography is likewise often defined as "the story of a life." But "story" is as unsatisfactory in its way as "record." As "record" implies sheer fact, "story" implies fiction. Story leads us away from actuality.

But if biography is not the history or the record or the story of a life, what of a life is it? Considering that biography represents imagination limited by truth, facts raised to the power of revelation, I suggest that it may be defined as "the simulation, in words, of a person's life, from all that is known about that person."

This concept of life-writing goes back to James Boswell. In a letter

why does kendall disagree with the Oxford definition?

40   to Bishop Percy he wrote, "It appears to me that mine is the best plan of biography that can be conceived; for my readers will, as near as may be, accompany Johnson in his progress, and, as it were, see each scene as it happened."

As the *simulation* in words of a life, biography works through effects, like the other literary arts; but it is an art with boundaries. The biographer, as Desmond McCarthy has felicitously pointed out, is "an artist upon oath." The definition excludes works at both ends of the biographical spectrum: the "fictionalized" biography simulates life but does not respect the materials at hand, whereas the fact-crammed biography, from the magpie school of scholarship-as-compilation, worships the materials at hand but does not simulate a life. The one fails truth; the other fails art. Between the two lies the impossible craft of true biography.

The shape of biography is partly created by the inner tensions peculiar to the practice. All great art achieves much of its force from tension, the exciting state of balance or reconciliation achieved among opposing elements. In painting there is obvious tension between form and color; in sculpture there is tension between the adamantine material and the plastic vision; in poetry there is tension between the violence of metaphor and the rigidity of meter.

Two characteristic tensions of biography arise out of the relation between the biographer and his subject and out of the conflict between the demands of simulation and the implacability of fact.

The question is often asked—how can a biographer be impartial (like a referee)? Of course, he cannot be so, would not be so. He is not a biologist looking at one-celled animals under the microscope, a curious but unmoved god. He is a human being deeply involved with another human being. He lives another life along with his own, and hopes he can persuade the reader to live that life along with *his* own. A biography may take a dozen years or more to write. Who would be willing, who would be able to spend that much time with a man for whom he had no feeling?

The biographer is forced into a struggle with his subject which is, in a way, the opposite of the novelist's struggle. The novelist must fight for detachment from material that is a part of him, so that he may see that material in aesthetic perspective, may ask it the right questions. The biographer is already detached from his material, but it is an inert, a fortuitous detachment, a detachment that has not been won but thrust upon him. Before he can achieve true detachment, he must first achieve something like the psychic immersion in his material that the novelist begins with.

In general, from the inception of modern life-writing in the fifteenth century to the present, the biographer, and the autobiographer too, have confronted their subjects with a sharpening consciousness of perils and possibilities. The deepening of psychological perception achieved in the twentieth century has affected the biographer's awareness of his relations with his materials as much as his understanding of the materials themselves.

A second, more obvious tension now develops between the subject, as brute materials, and the writer, as shaping intelligence; the conflict between the intransigence of facts and the imperious demand of art. It is this second tension that I have been mindful of in my definition of biography as the simulation, in words, of a life—but a simulation growing out of the materials at hand.

The researcher yearns to secure every scrap of paper left by a man's life; it is the artist who reminds him that he must stop somewhere—or death will take him as he stoops for yet another clue, and he will leave no mark of his struggles, except disorderly file boxes for his widow to dispose of. All the time that the biographer is collecting these scraps of paper, he must be doing something about them. At best, fact is harsh, recalcitrant matter, as tangible as the hunk of rusty iron one trips over and yet as shapeless as a paper hat in the rain. Fact is a cold stone, an inarticulate thing, dumb until something happens to it; and there is no use the biographer waiting for spontaneous combustion or miraculous alchemy. Fact must be rubbed up in the mind, placed in magnetic juxtaposition with other facts, until it begins to glow, to give off that radiance we call meaning. Fact is a biographer's only friend, and worst enemy.

This delicate adjustment between evidence and interpretation is partly determined by the way in which the biographer solves his problems, the problems indigenous to his material, and the general problems that confront all biographers. Like the other arts, biography has its cross-play of peculiar opportunities and dangers, and the quality of biography is largely determined by the biographer's ability to meet these challenges.

When biographers talk shop among themselves, you will hear animated discussions of a problem rarely mentioned by reviewers, the problem of gaps. That paper trail, extending from the birth certificate to the death certificate, is never continuous or complete. The more remote in time the subject is, the more gaps there will be.

These gaps occur at all stages in the trail but are very likely to come during the childhood and adolescence of the subject. One of the great triumphs of Boswell is the consummate biographical tact with which he resolved gaps. He spent less than a year—scattered over several years—in Johnson's company, and whereas he had masses of material for the later part of Johnson's life, he had comparatively thin materials for the earlier part. Yet he succeeds in giving the reader a sense of Johnson's life unfolding, a sense of that life being lived, from the beginning to the end.

There are no rules for handling gaps. Each paper trail is unlike any other paper trail. Each biographer is unlike any other biographer. The right way to fill gaps is unknown; the wrong ways are legion.[1]

Confronting a gap, the writer can but recognize that he is domesticated in imperfection; at the same time he must respond to King Harry's call—"Once more into the breach!"—and, summoning his talents and honesty, struggle to suggest the life of his man during the blank, without either pretending to more knowledge than he has or breaking the reader's illusion of a life unfolding.

I will use an experience of my own only because it is accessible. In trying to write a biography of Richard III, I was faced with an enormous gap in Richard's boyhood. From the age of ten till about fifteen (1462–66) he is but the merest supernumerary in the annals of the time. I could find only three elements out of which to build a bridge: what-was-going-on-in-England; what, in all probability, he was doing; where he was living.

Since Richard's brother, King Edward IV, and the mighty king-maker, Richard, earl of Warwick, were in these years moving toward a collision in which Richard would be deeply involved, the great

---

[1]I recently chanced to look at four biographies of Francis Bacon: Charles Williams, *Bacon*, n.d.; Mary Sturt, *Francis Bacon*, 1932; Bryan Bevan, *The Real Francis Bacon*, 1960; Catherine Drinker Bowen, *Francis Bacon: The Temper of a Man*, 1963:
Little is known about Bacon's formative years: he went to Cambridge at thirteen; his later teens he spent in the train of the English ambassador to France; he then studied law at Gray's Inn. The writer has only about half a dozen biographical elements with which to fill this lamentable gap in Bacon's youth: information about his father, the Lord Keeper, and his mother; descriptions of the Bacon town and country houses; the state of learning at Cambridge; the political-cultural situation in France; life in the Inns of Court; and "background of the age." Each of the four biographers emphasizes one or more of these elements; it is not altogether clear, however, in the first three biographies whether that emphasis derives from quantity of material available, its attractiveness to the author, or its importance in Bacon's life. Mrs. Bowen steers the most decisive course by giving an over-all thematic significance to Bacon's youth, seeing it as the years of his "Eden," before he discovered, on the death of his father, that for all his high connections he would have to make his own way in the world.

events of the period had to be intertwined in the texture of his life. I sought to introduce them, not from Richard's viewpoint—which would mean a leap into a mind closed to me—nor yet as inert information interrupting the biography, but as the stuff of Richard's developing experience.

As for the other elements, I had only the naked fact that Richard was being schooled as a "henxman," or page, in the household of the earl of Warwick at Middleham Castle in Wensleydale, Yorkshire.

Out of several contemporary "courtesy books" and a mercifully detailed manual on the proper education for an aspirant knight, I sought to reconstruct the probable pattern of Richard's boyhood days. Place itself provided equally valuable clues. On the southern slope of Wensleydale—a great rift in the Yorkshire moors through which tumbles the river Ure—there stand the massive ruins of Middleham Castle. Behind, the land rolls up to the sky; before, stretch the village and the valley; then, empty moorland climbing to the clouds. It was in Richard's day a wild sweep of country, inhabited by a folk more primitive than those in Edward IV's capital, marked by huge stone abbeys and bristling castles, the hills rounded by the stamp of Celtic kings and Roman legions. Since, in later years, Richard owned Middleham and spent his happiest days there, I concluded that he must have developed his feeling for the region during his early sojourn. I therefore juxtaposed his training in knighthood with an account of Wensleydale and its people in an attempt to suggest the shape of his boyhood.

The problem of filling gaps involves more than material; it is likewise a question of rhythm. Obviously, the amount of biographical space-time devoted to a moment in the subject's life should approximate the weight of significance of the moment. Not only, then, must the writer find material in the things that stand around, in order to bridge space; he must likewise sensitively adjust the movement of the narrative so that its pace reflects the true pace of the life. Otherwise, even the least perceptive reader will feel that "something is wrong," perhaps that the biography is "dry" or that the biographer has somehow cheated him or that he has missed a point. When the narrative moves quickly or slowly according to the quantity of the material rather than the quality of the experience, the writer *and* his subject have become prisoners of the papers.

It is gaps that tempt the fledgling biographer to speculate, the "artistic" biographer to invent, the scholarly biographer to give a lecture on history. To fill gaps by wondering aloud, lying, padding—or

44 simply to leave them for the reader to tumble into—is not to fill the shoes of a true biographer.

If the absence of witnesses—gaps—poses one of the chief biographical problems, availability of witnesses does not mean that the biographer can switch on the automatic pilot. Mark Schorer has eloquently commented on the vanity, fallibility, unconscious duplicity, animosity, taciturnity or volubility of living witnesses and evoked the specter of libel rustling above the workbench of the biographer writing of a man recently deceased, like Sinclair Lewis.

Dead witnesses, preserved only as paper, are no less humanly perverse, inaccurate, and prejudiced; and if they have been dead for more than two centuries, their terseness, their indifference to details of behavior, their maddening penchant for generalizing, moralizing, and sometimes paralyzing human situations, in sum, their over-all failure to satisfy the most modest demands of twentieth-century curiosity, offer perhaps even greater obstacles to biography than the copiousness, however misleading, of the witness-in-the-flesh.

This brief sketch of some of the enigmas that beset the biographical workshop is no place for a discussion of the lenses to be employed in the scrutiny of evidences. Rules have been promulgated in a few manuals of life-writing, but I suspect that they represent not so much an analytic account of the battle in progress as a picture of the terrain after the dead have been buried, the field tidied, and historical markers erected. The bald truth is, however "scientifically" the biographer tries to quiz his witnesses, he is often sloppy, intuitive, temerarious, doubt-ridden, and hopeful, his intellect clouded by visceral irrelevancies and glandular dreams. In short, he is a frail mortal, on a very mortal mission, measuring other frail mortals. If he pretends to be a microscope, the damned specimen evaporates.

Judicial, scientific, historical tests of evidence are useful, but the writer who deals in the unstable stuff of letters, diary, conversations, hearsay, the elusiveness of human testimony not offered as testimony, evidences that may yield more in their lies, omissions, euphemisms, and periphrases than in their truths, mainly depends on his shaky knowledge of psychology, his own sense of human nature, what he has learned from other biographers, dogged industry, a skepticism that is quizzical rather than systematic, and a determination to reject the golden fable for the leaden fact.

The biographer does not trust his witnesses, living or dead. He may drip with the milk of human kindness, believe everything that his wife and his friends and his children tell him, enjoy his neighbors and embrace the universe—but in the workshop he must be as ruthless as a board meeting smelling out embezzlement, as suspicious as a secret agent riding the Simplon-Orient express, as cold-eyed as a pawnbroker viewing a leaky concertina. With no respect for human dignity, he plays off his witnesses one against the other, snoops for additional information to confront them with, probes their prejudices and their pride, checks their reliability against their self-interest, thinks the worst until he is permitted to think better. Withal, he must expect to be deceived, and more than once, and thus stand ready, unto page proof, to excise the much tested truth that turns out to be error or invention.

The biographer attempting to make sense out of the imperfect paper trail, brooding over gaps and gabble, is like a man sitting at a bizarre play. He knows the "plot" and the cast of characters, and he understands substantially what is going to happen. His mission, however, is to report the drama in detail; of which the performance he is witnessing is a flawed and sometimes zany simulacrum.

Happenings explode on the stage without warning; happenings are prepared for and fail to occur; supporting players pop up with nothing to do and disappear into the wings when most needed. The protagonist is supposed to be always on stage; but he sometimes vanishes, even in the middle of a speech, or crawls into a corner when the script clearly calls for him to stand front and center, or exhibits inexplicable postures of agony or joy, or at a critical moment falls suddenly silent. Actions move toward a climax which is cut off by a descending curtain; important exchanges between characters take place behind the furniture; and on occasion the subsidiary actors maliciously mask the protagonist and carry on a Hamletless *Hamlet*.

Sometimes the biographer cannot hear; sometimes he cannot see; sometimes he cannot understand what he does hear and see. Yet, by means of this performance he must re-create the play—without inventing anything and without altering the plot.

Another of the great biographical problems is the management of time. A novel usually pictures only a segment of life; the novelist shuttles forward and backward in time in order to enrich that segment; the fictional character is a creature of the novelist's time. But a person is a creature of actual time; we must be able to share with him not only the grand human chronology of growth, maturity,

46   death, but also lesser patterns of sequential experience, small half-hidden cumulations of behavior from which emerge new tendrils of relationship between the man and his world.

In the earlier drafts of a biography of King Louis XI on which I am still working, I succumbed to a fictional device for the opening. The shape of the materials themselves and the opportunity to sketch immediately the chief theme of Louis's youth prompted me to manipulate time like a novelist.

Not until his thirteenth year, as a bridegroom, does Louis make a sustained appearance in history. Contemporary chronicles describe the wedding in sufficient detail so that I could mold the materials into a scene, place Louis at the center of a cluster of moments. Even better, the behavior of Louis's father, Charles VII, at the ceremony revealed his hostility toward the boy; and it was a bitter antagonism between father and son that was to shape Louis's whole life as dauphin.

Thus, by beginning with Louis at thirteen instead of at birth, I plunged the reader at once into a life being lived, and provided a focus for the first twelve years of his life—which I then recounted—in the unspoken question: what had caused, so early, bad feeling between king and dauphin?

Though doubts soon assailed me, I clung to this pretty opening through several drafts. No use: I had to junk it. A character in a novel inhabits a time-dimension invented by the author and has no existence apart from it. A person, however, has his own time-dimension, quite independent of a biographer's ingenuity. In rupturing Louis's time to impose my own, I was turning him into a fictional being, I was overtly staging rather than unfolding a life.

So Louis himself kept imperiously reminding me. I was, he told me, foisting on the public *my* Louis instead of him, *the* Louis. Furthermore, I was cutting him off from his common humanity: like other human beings he began as a baby, not as a bridegroom. He declared rudely that if I had so little confidence in his identity as an actual person, there was no use my trying to accompany him through a lifetime.

I have let him have his way: he begins by being born, and I end a little wiser. Biographical time and novelistic time do not mix.

Yet biography is the simulation, not the ledger book, of an existence. The biographer cannot reproduce the actual concatenation of events. His subject may, over a period of months, be developing a dozen different themes of experience; if the biographer attempts to thread the tangle of details day by day out of which these experiences are being built he will conjure up chaos. He must thrust into the reader's ears the noisy crosscurrents of man's passage through time, wet his tongue with the salty murk of reality; but if he is to make that passage intelligible, he must do violence to time: the clutter of events will be cut away, happenings scattered through years will be grouped, in order to reveal underlying currents of behavior.

Certain continuing sounds in the "buzz and hum" of daily life—a hobby, an eccentricity of diet, a habitual inability to stay awake at lectures, a desultory friendship too important to omit but insufficiently substantial to be woven through—will almost of necessity be grouped arbitrarily and brought into the narrative when the biographer's ear tells him that the moment has struck. The chief purpose of "groupings," however, is to elicit—but not to diagram—the master-themes of a life: patterns of hopes and illusions, preoccupations, fears, rhythmic movements of character discernible in the diurnal stream of existence, grand designs of personality expressed as behavior.

Yet thematic groupings cannot be permitted to block or deform the sweep of chronology, the sequential heart-beat of a life, the "faring onward" of our tragi-comic journey. They cannot be deployed like the topics of an expository essay—exposition is the enemy of biography, dead tissue cumbering a living organism. They must suggest a life moving through time, not the writer's capacity for tidiness. James Parton, the first American professional biographer, put the matter practically: "A good thing is twice as good if it comes in at the right place."

Suetonius and Plutarch, working in the narrow compass of sketch, or profile, developed a biographical mode in which thematic grouping and the unfolding of time interpenetrated each other in a stylized arrangement of life-materials. Certain present-day biographers have sauced the device of "grouping" with psychoanalysis and novelistic legerdemain as if human chronology were as boneless as an oyster and a life so much mud to be arbitrarily patted into cakes.

The absence, or the prevalence, of witnesses, gaps and traps in the paper trail, the management of time, and the eliciting of patterns are some of the most difficult challenges confronting a biographer. I will mention but one more, the problem of balancing the time-viewpoint of the subject and the time-viewpoint of the biographer. It is easy to

48   see that what is the unknown future for the subject is the well-known past for the biographer; and it is easy to say that the biographer must use the advantage of this difference but not take advantage of it.

In practice, however, the distinction between re-creating and commenting on a life is not so easy to respect. And the distinction is one that must be dealt with at the most critical moments in the life, the moments of decision, the moment when career takes a turn or love takes a wife, the moment when character is simultaneously illustrated and reshaped by a choice of action or attitude. These are the moments, sometimes not simple to detect, which mark the true stages of existence, the determining and determinate climaxes summing up the past and giving birth to the future, the moments when, as Carlyle pointed out, a man (and his biographer) discovers what he is in what he does.

Inevitably, then, the biographer seeks to choose, in the welter of psychological-physical happenings leading toward such a moment, those elements which will be crucial in the subject's decision, as, after the moment, he must bring into the foreground those elements which show the working out of the decision. To such an extent the biographer, thanks to his vantage point in time, can comment upon the life.

But biographers are sometimes tempted to comment overtly on the decision itself, before it is made, after it is made, even as it is being made. They shout at Napoleon that he must not send Grouchy in pursuit of Blucher, at Hamilton that he had better steer clear of Burr, at James that it is idle for him to attempt the drama, at Antony that he is foolish to fight by sea, at Ben Jonson that he should not try to compose classical tragedy—and the deafened reader cannot hear what is actually going on, is jerked away from the subject to the biographer; indeed, the deafened reader is likely to conclude, perhaps unfairly, that the biographer is arrogantly pluming himself on a prescience that has no more merit than the good luck of being born considerably later than his subject.

If the biographer is to create the sense of a life being lived, he cannot leap from his own time into his subject's time to nudge the poor man in the ribs or make faces at his deliberations, like Faustus playing tricks on the pope. The grand dimension of every man's life is the opacity of the future. The biographer, if he has foresight, will exercise the willing suspension of hindsight.

Biography attempts the simulation, in words, of a person's life, from what is known about that life, from the paper trail, the enigmatic footprint. Thus it differs from other literary arts. They seek to evoke reality from illusion; biography hopes to fasten illusion upon reality, to elicit, from the coldness of paper, the warmth of a life being lived.

Four

Biography as an Agent of Humanism

How could biography be anything but an agent of humanism? The title of this essay seems to be sufficient for the message. Yet there are too many meanings of both biography and humanism to justify an urge to avoid talking for a decent moment on a subject of tantalizing dimensions.

Biography as a literary genre has undergone a sea change in this century. From the ancients' moral lesson to Victorian elegiac to Freudian revelation to modern life re-creation—so runs the history of biography. But the roads to the present in life-writing are various, and the varieties confusing indeed.

Humanism, too, boasts a checkered history. By definition, humanism is a complex variable. According to the *Oxford English Dictionary*, humanism embraces "belief in the mere humanity of Christ," "any system of thought or action which is concerned with merely human interests (as distinguished from divine)," and also "devotion to those studies which promote human culture." By usage, "humanism" was the label given to the new study of Greek and Roman antiquities that sparked the Renaissance. Recently humanism has come to serve an especially malign purpose—as whipping boy for the New Right. Seizing on that part of the definition which speaks of "belief in the mere humanity of Christ," New Right demagogues seek to smear one of the finest scholarly traditions with their own conception of a horrid agnosticism. So humanism is certainly a useful term.

What, from all these possibilities, am I going to talk about? I propose to speak of art and empathy; I want to look at biography as an art form and at humanism as the "character of being human"—really as a special quality that quickens human clay.

One simile above all others recurs in writing about biography— the comparison of biographers with portraitists. From Plutarch to André Maurois to Barbara W. Tuchman biographers have remarked the kinship they feel with portrait painters. And the analogy is apt, for biography can range in scope from a sketch—a pencil outline—to a full, total account—a large canvas; and biography can be written in small segments—in light brushstrokes—or in a variety of layers—shadings—or even in overwhelming totality—say, the Hudson River treatment! Most important is that both forms of art aim at the same purpose: to illuminate reality.

All biographers know the need to build their subject's life through time and career, know the need to layer in details and traits as time shapes a nature. Pundits and popular psychologists speak glibly of "passages" in human lives; biographers would generally welcome so simple a solution to problems of maturation and change. They know all too well that formulas cannot substitute for facts, that personalities differ, that reactions stem from sources which refuse easy listing, and that people gleefully defy pigeonholes.

Biographers, because they have some perception of people, are a peculiar lot. In some ways they remind me of George Santayana's historian—as, at one and the same time, the highest and lowest of creatures. The historian fitted that definition because he would know so much about his subject that he would be inundated. "Such knowledge," said philosopher Santayana, "must dissolve thought in a vertigo if it has not already perished of boredom."

All biographers must steep themselves in data, work with those data for some time, let them work on them, and then begin to pick and choose what they perceive as necessary to shape a person from the past—more than that, to evoke a person into being.

Evocation of personality, of character, is the highest biographical art. Description, analysis even, can come without evocation, but when a person seems to come off the pages in full force, then the biographer has truly succeeded. That kind of witchery follows great familiarity with a subject's times and contemporaries, problems, travails, triumphs, loves, and losses. To achieve that kind of immersion, a biographer must live with a subject, in fact, must go back into time and a life and walk old footprints—walk in another's moccasins, in American Indian parlance.

All things that touched the subject—people, artifacts, papers, memoirs, oddments of costume, fancies, speeches, recordings, writings—are the biographer's clay. And they are not inert, these dry scripts and shards; they guide a writer's pen and often subdue a scholar's wish. Beyond the remains—beyond what I call the existential evidence—there is another layer of evidence that no biographer can ignore. This layer—which, for want of a better term, I call the "secondary evidence" (Leon Edel calls it the "psychological evidence")—constitutes the meanings, appreciations, nuances of character that can be deduced from the existential evidence and from traits and habits. Both layers are vital, both available only after hard research.

Evidence is, of course, the main ingredient in life-writing. But mere massing of data is no guarantee of evocation. Biographers have to provide the final human ingredient of translation. And as they study what they have discovered, as they ply the business of evocation, they must be on guard against external conditions that may warp their work.

Every discipline endures various fads—biography and history are no exceptions. As new ideas and techniques in science and social science developed, some historians and biographers tried to use them in penetrating the past. Especially has this been true with regard to science—in part, I think, because scientists have become the magicians of our time. Social science followed along as fast as possible, seeking to graft onto the great cornucopia in Washington. Among the new tools that appear especially useful to studies of people is, of course, psychology. Although psychology suffers cross doctrines and quarreling theories, historians and biographers have seized on it and plunged into analyses of hidden motives, disturbed libidos, unbalanced minds. Results have been mixed, at least to me. Sigmund Freud and William C. Bullitt wrote a psychological study of Woodrow Wilson that hardly charmed reviewers and, in fact, seemed to underscore a telling comment by Emile Durkheim to the effect that history could be used to elucidate psychology but never the reverse. Psychoanalysis can aid the biographer, but only when skillfully handled.

There is another facet of science that some biographers tie to—and that crosses psychoanalysis with biology. This branch of biography is sometimes called biopsychology or dynamic psychology and is well illustrated by Robert W. White's *Lives in Progress: A Study in the Natural Growth of Personality*. White's passion is to elucidate "natural growth of personality," that is, the development through time of nonaberrant psyches. His case studies make good reading and emphasize the biographer's need to portray a subject's growth and development, to paint a life in maturing stages of change.

Social science, too, charms biography. Sociology helps life-writing, but not directly. So far, sociology tends to talk of societies, of large numbers, of groups rather than individuals. Economics toys with laws, and political science focuses on the behavior of voters and governments at various levels. Anthropology, by its very nature, broadens its lens to whole peoples in the past. Archaeology comes closest to history and biography in its impartial acceptance of artifacts left by one or by many.

In recent years all social sciences have been heavily influenced by psychology. Most of them are grouped under the umbrella name "behavioral sciences," since they study mass reaction and motivation. Some historians and biographers cherish the behaviorist label and would wave it proudly over their books and papers. But the main body of biography still clings to individuality, still seeks to know how one man or woman lived and worked in his or her time, how one life may have influenced many.

Lest I be accused of ignoring a rich contributory stream, let me mention a growing interest among some historians in group studies. Such outstanding scholars as George F. Rudé, with *The Crowd in History*, and Richard C. Cobb, with *Death in Paris* and *Paris and Its Provinces*, have extended the dimensions of group psychology and discovered a collective personality that promises new and greater insight into man.

And now there are whole categories of normally "silent" people emerging from obscurity because of recent approaches to research that shift biographical perception. I am referring to Richard Cobb's study of a single class of French workers—personal servants— whose opinions about their employers, their nation, and the world change what we know of prerevolutionary Europe. These people are articulate now because new approaches to evidence lifted the cloak of obscurity and gave them life.

A new trend toward psychoanalytical biographies fogged in jargon is altogether dismal. Jargon has taken over much writing in the social sciences. Obscurantism marches on!

I have noticed an interesting contrast in historical or biographical works about science or scientists written by scientists. These studies are often models of clarity. Consider such recent works as Daniel J. Kevles's *The Physicists* or Elof Axel Carlson's *Hermann J. Muller*. Donald Clayton, a Rice space physicist, writes gracefully of the cosmos. So, too, does mathematician E. T. Bell write fascinatingly about his colleagues, in *Men of Mathematics*. Isaac Asimov is perhaps the best-known science fictioner—and is no mean scientist. Precision is not the only hallmark of scientists as writers about their colleagues and their fields—they pull readers into their subjects with strong, muscular prose, and they tell good stories. At any rate, most of them avoid jargon.

Can the same be said of historians and biographers—do they write crisply of their kind and field? Large collective works on historiography lack literary distinction. James Thomson Shotwell's *History of History* is interesting but fairly typical collective biography—a book that assesses rather than evokes—and that is not a criticism, since Shotwell's aim is not to do biography but to analyze contributions made by various scholars. Michael Kraus's *History of American History* strikes me as more critical and less interesting than Shotwell's larger work.

Biographers have hacked away at their colleagues with gusto. Boswell has his Frederick Pottle, but, in general, biographers suffer from collective analysis or in essays done in dudgeon by collegial reviewers. A great many of them come to the surface for a line or two in how-to books on biography, usually examples of how-not-to! There is a healthy kind of jealousy abroad in the biographical world—the kind that spurs and spites and stimulates—and has, I think, elevated the genre.

A good deal of fine writing, though, has been done by biographers about biography. Like Leon Edel or not, he writes engagingly and with feeling about how to write another's life. I personally disagree with 98 percent of his well-selling *Literary Biography* but confess its charm and persuasion. André Maurois's *Aspects of Biography* suits my taste more happily, and here, again, is an artist limning his art. If I were asked my favorite work about biography, I would name instantly Paul Murray Kendall's *The Art of Biography*. There is nothing pious in it; it simply says more about a biographer's obligations and explains more about a biographer's problems in a few pages than can be found in countless tomes on writing. Kendall is a distinguished biographer. Experience lends an extra dimension to his discussion of research, technique, and evocation. Only one who has suffered the toils of wringing a human being from the mists could so well describe the value of seeing and knowing places that a subject walked or knew. Kendall has called Louis XI from long ago, has brought the "spider King" to sparking life—and has done it because he lived with him, touched his bones, and walked in his swirling dust.

Kendall believes, as do Veronica Wedgwood and many others, that he must go where his subject went to share feelings and to know a personality. He says: "The interaction of biographer and subject is heightened by the biographer's direct, sensory experience of the matrix from which the subject's experience has been shaped. The biographer opens himself to all that places and things will tell him, in his struggle to visualize, and to sense, his man in being." Real knowledge of a subject demands more: "Deepest of all, the particular kind of biographer of whom I am speaking, cherishes, I believe, a conviction—call it a romantic quirk, if you will—that where the subject has trod he must tread, what the subject has seen he must see, because he thus achieves an indefinable but unmistakable kinship with his man." In personal terms, Kendall confesses that "it would be vain for me to assert that the biography of Louis XI . . . will be demonstrably abler because I have held in my hand—within the whispering vault by Cléry, the church he built—the massive skull which still, by the language of sheer bone, bespeaks the marvelously ugly countenance of that consummate actor." He believes, though, that places do tell things to biographers. He says that on a visit to Louis's battlefield at Montlhéry, where the king waged, "under circumstances which dramatically reveal the motions of his character, a wild, bloody battle with his mortal foe, Charles of Burgundy, I believe that I learned more than the physical appearance of terrain and the probable movements of the armies." And the sight of the field on a July day much like the one of battle made an impression to carry beyond the moment into art: "There stood fields of wheat and beans shimmering in the sun, there lay the village canted on the hillside, and at my back, gray stone walls of the royal castle. Perhaps I am deceived in thinking that what then happened to me was more than a *frisson*, a literary thrill. I can but report that I felt a shock of recognition, a poignant apprehension of Louis that I had not previously achieved."

What will happen to works such as Kendall's, works in the literary tradition, if science and pseudoscience lock hold on biography? They will vanish in a mass of statistics, in a maze of models and computer printouts. That thought brings a dismal image of a day when books are themselves artifacts, all reading is done on consoles, and biography is offered by regression analysis and probability theory.

Of course, by now you know that I like literary biography—if not in the Edel sense! It is, I know, often criticized as old-fashioned, as a throwback to Lytton Strachey, even to Suetonius and Plutarch. Modern practitioners like Edel, and many in the psychological school, argue that literary biographies lack new perceptions and depths and are tied too closely to imagination. These allegations are partly true and partly false. Biography as literature has really come into its own in this century. Strachey blew open the genre with *Eminent Victorians,* followed by his artful *Life of Queen Victoria.* Clearly style and content could mix, and biography could be stimulating social history as well as life simulation. All kinds of avenues were tried, from a new kind of autobiographical approach that accepted fiction within its confines (Robert Graves's *I, Claudius* is a fine example) to the openly fictionalized life (Catherine Drinker Bowen's *Yankee from Olympus* ranks at the top).

Scholarly biography, long viewed askance by readers and publishers, had caught a large segment of the popular market by the mid-1950s. Although Albert J. Beveridge's *John C. Marshall* (1916–19) had long loomed over American biography, it seemed more a landmark than a beacon. It was the happy blend of subject and biographer that opened the way for scholarly writers to take honorable place at biography's table. An editor at Scribner's decided in the early 1920s that the market might stand a one-volume life of Robert E. Lee. He asked a young Virginian, Douglas Southall Freeman, to write it. Freeman had published a large collection of Lee letters and had gained wide renown as a rising scholar at Johns Hopkins University. Freeman worked for almost twenty years and produced four large volumes. Despite its bulk, despite the frighteningly careful research reflected in an awesome array of footnotes, *R. E. Lee: A Biography* immediately set new standards for literature, scholarship, and biography. It stands as a perennial model for biographies.

Freeman's background—his own biography—lent strength to his work. A newspaperman, he wrote daily, knew how to find facts and how to use them. Residence in Richmond gave him an entree to sources kept for the faithful, and his own upbringing etched the value of character. Lee emerged from Freeman's pages a graceful, gentle man with a romance running deep in the blood—a romance that could rage and make a tall, courtly soldier a fiery man of war. What Freeman brought to his task proved vital.

Other examples of modern biographical literature abound. Stephen Oates writes as I would like to write. The late T. Harry Williams, famed for his *Huey Long,* wrote with equal grace and perhaps even deeper understanding in *Lincoln and His Generals.* Confederate general P. G. T. Beauregard also caught his attention, and *Napoleon in Gray* is still the best on the subject. Williams is worth more consideration; he wrote two kinds of biography—of one and of many. And he did both with gusto. Research was a hallmark, but style was his forte. His books will linger as primers of organization, method, and presentation.

Sinclair Lewis, that prodigious literary force, has attracted one of the best biographies of our age—the massive study by Mark Schorer. I confess to having had only a slight interest in Lewis, but once beyond the title page of Schorer's book, I was caught—caught as much by the biography as by the subject. So artful, insightful, so crafted are Schorer's pages that they pull the reader into Lewis's life, ready or not. That kind of biography poses, I think, a fascinating question: How true to life is it? Is the subject made by the book? It can happen, of course—a book can drag its theme to greatness. In biography, however, that kind of alchemy, it seems to me, is dangerous. Not that I think that the subject should overwhelm the biographer—far from it. I do think, though, that a subject should command respect, admiration, or total damnation on his or her own merits. Cast to the future in false dimension may sometimes seem a happy prospect, but not really. A man or woman deserves his or her own size and merits, and biographers have an obligation not to distort, willfully or otherwise.

That demand for dimensional accuracy hampers biographers' imagination and, in some ways, levies a harsher burden than even historians carry. Both biographers and historians honor facts; biographers honor, too, personality and character and must do no violence to either.

In their quest for responsible accuracy, life-writers now deploy far more tools for rummaging in the past than ever before. Science, of course, aids, abets, and sometimes curses, along with social science. New dimensions of social history often help us see a subject in proper surroundings. Art, music, theater—each offers a glimpse at interests, perhaps even motivation.

In the reaches of mass biography, history touches closely—and the touch seems to reinforce the old assertion that biography is the handmaiden of history. Barbara W. Tuchman, in a graceful essay entitled "Biography as a Prism of History," says that, as a prism, biography "attracts and holds the reader's interest in the larger subject. People are interested in other people, in the fortunes of the individual." Biography is also attractive, Tuchman thinks, "because it encompasses the universal in the particular. It is a focus that allows both the writer to narrow his field to manageable dimensions and the reader to more easily comprehend the subject. . . . the artist, as

Frank E. Vandiver

58   Robert Frost once said, needs only a sample. One does not try for the whole but for what is truthfully *representative*."

To my mind collective biography is one of the most difficult and useful branches of the life-writing art. Tuchman uses it skillfully in her wide-ranging histories; historians often use the biographical sketch to highlight an age with a person. There have been, and are, biographers who offer whole sets of sketches as the best avenue to understanding people, place, and time. Plutarch's *Parallel Lives* was deftly honed to intrigue readers while teaching them ethics. Writing, though, ranked high with Plutarch. He knew the value of attracting an audience. His sketches still read well, and the ethics intrude little enough as lives parade from an ancient world. Gamaliel Bradford's "psychographs" added attraction to the field as they followed Strachey's new wave. Bradford's work I find useful yet; his *Union Portraits* and *Confederate Portraits* show his knack of quick evocation—a style and art worth continuing. Hendrik Willem Van Loon's *Lives* is another venture into the sketcher's realm—again, the results are intriguing and set character and person easily in time and place.

I have saved Strachey's *Eminent Victorians* for a special word. Graceful, "lacquered" style, skilled insights, willingness to shake traditions willy-nilly, sometimes scalding wit, all contained in Strachey's work, set new directions for life-writing. He broke idols. Biography had, in his time, languished in a kind of filiopietistic moralism that inundated readers in undigested facts interlined with preachy praise of the subject. Hardly an art, biography survived simply because it still boasted people for its topic.

Strachey boasted people when he thought it right. He damned them when they deserved damning, and he damned his biographical colleagues who strung facts together without a care for art. Large, two-volume lives he hated: "They are as familiar as the *cortège* of the undertaker, and wear the same air of slow, funeral barbarism." For him these granite tomes taught lessons: "To preserve . . . a becoming brevity—a brevity which excludes everything that is redundant and nothing that is significant. . . . To maintain his (the biographer's) own freedom of spirit. It is not his business to be complimentary, it is his business to lay bare the facts of the case as he understands them."

Strachey's iconoclasm brought respectability to life-writing and ushered in human foibles as legitimate concerns. His work did much for the sketchers, who could at last limn their subjects as people, not as icons. The eminent Victorians who throng Strachey's pages show sketching as a higher art. Not long, the sketches are nimble, graceful, witty, and caustic, and they charm because they persuade. From that model stem the many clusters of lives I have mentioned before.

There is another cachet approach in biography: the dictionary school. Dictionaries are not new; they have enjoyed scholarly gratitude for more than a century. *Larousse, The Dictionary of National Biography, Appleton's*—these are traditionals. Of them all I think that *The Dictionary of American Biography* sets an unmatched tone of style and content. First under the guidance of Dumas Malone, an eminent biographer of Jefferson, then under John A. Garraty, this distinguished series continues to raise new standards. And who is to argue that there is not more useful history in such a compilation than in all the history books? At least, with my prejudices, I find history there especially palatable.

Which leads back to the matter of biography as a handmaiden of history. I would argue that both are handmaidens of each other. Whether or not you agree with Thomas Carlyle and the "great man" theory of history, you must concede that people do make history. People even shape some of the so-called great forces that seem immutable—economics, for example.

I am intrigued by the part that human reactions play in shaping history—especially human accommodation to events over which people have no control. Acts of God demand man's response: great storms that kill thousands bring human palliation; shifting ground and sweeping plagues produce reactions that, in themselves, create history. These reactions deserve more biographical magnification.

In my own particular area, military history, biography is unusually important—and I would really like to call myself a military biographer rather than a military historian. I say that biography is important in the study of military affairs because the careers of great captains do loom above the mass of lives—and in the careers of these men can often be glimpsed lessons for younger leaders. Why? Because the art of war resembles other arts—techniques and practices, skills and applications vary in various hands, but the true artist creates personal rules.

Biography is important, too, in the military realm because it forces concentration on specific human qualities instead of on operations, intelligence, logistics, training—all the details of war administration. All great philosophers and commentators on war have remarked on a trait that is shared by great captains, one trait that separates the true leader from other ranks: character. Definitions of the quality vary, yet there is general acceptance of some elements common to superior battle commanders. Physical courage they all share, a touch of fatalism, too, that lends deliberateness to their deeds, and most of all a way of sticking, a firmness not given to many as battles shift and sway, a sense of purpose and resolve that carries out to their soldiers and creates optimism. Commentators from the ancient Chinese Sun Tzu to General Maxwell Taylor remark the need for character. If they all perceive it differently, they all concede its grace. Great captains who have it are not always the bravest, not always the glorious—but they have an honesty bred that gives trust in their orders and faith in their plans. Character, that elusive mark of honor, is the luminous hallmark of great soldiers from Miltiades to Douglas MacArthur.

What is it about character that so entices admiration? It is, for one thing, the quality that seems to sift the few from the rest. Those who stand the test of truth and perseverance are celebrated—witness Winston Churchill on Marlborough, virtually hundreds on Napoleon, Freeman on Lee, John Wheeler-Bennett on Hindenburg, Anthony Nutting on T. E. Lawrence, Forrest C. Pogue on George C. Marshall. Character is often revealed in war reminiscences—those specialities of autobiography most artfully contributed by beaten commanders. The good ones show their strength of will, their devotion to victory, their dedication to the right course; bad ones reveal weakness through convenient memories and quick resort to blame.

Biographers lucky enough to live for some time in the company of a character sense a change in their own lives. I noted with pleasure Stephen Oates's remark that "I may have re-created Martin Luther King's life, but he changed mine." I share that feeling after five years' companionship with Stonewall Jackson and an eighteen years' trek after Black Jack Pershing.

Is human character an essential ingredient in history? I think so. And, if that is so, are biography and history separable?

They are separable, I think, only in the minds of students of the "laws of history," those scholars who put people at the bottom of the historical spectrum. The two fields are interdependent. In the works of Edward Gibbon and Michael I. Rostovtzeff, Thomas Carlyle and Lytton Strachey, Arnold Toynbee and Alexander Solzhenitsyn, Romain Rolland and Sir Winston Churchill, the genres blend.

Even though they blend, more readers flock to lives than to histories. Why? There is the obvious answer: People like to read about people. But is there something more, some intangible quality in written lives that attracts? Let me speak in my own terms about the biographer's business to see whether a discussion of the nature of the craft may reveal some hidden lure.

I think that biography—and I use the word to mean a study of someone no longer alive—is history made personal. Good biographies deal with the ways people faced living—tell how they met problems, how they coped with big and little crises, how they loved, competed, did the things we all do daily—and hence these studies touch familiar chords in readers.

Modern research techniques lend some new attractions to biography. As scholars use new tools to probe the past, even to plumb psyches, a multidimensional figure emerges from the sources. Social history perhaps adds an especially appealing facet to life-writing by the perspective it throws on the times of lives. Computer analysis can make easier the counting of monies and votes and even give a hint at probabilities—if the biographer dares to take the hint. Tape recorders offer recollections of a subject's contemporaries.

These new tools are added to the old and simply enlarge the biographer's sternest test—to select, arrange, organize the mass of data and conjure life from leavings. Here is where the "art" of the writer is tested: How witch from disparate sources not only the shape but also the actions of a subject and simulate a person? Whether or not a living being walks off the pages depends wholly on the biographer's skill as artist, conjurer, creator.

If evocation happens, it happens not by magic or by mirrors but by hard work. The biographer must live with a subject until he or she becomes real, until the writer shares a life. The result will not be a memoir, no matter how real the subject may seem, for the veil of existence cannot be broken, but it will be a study touched with empathy. I am convinced that no honest biographer—as opposed to the propagandist or the avowed debunker—can long remain in company and consort with a subject and avoid at least a touch of empathy.

Empathy is biography's quintessential quality—without it lives are mere chronicles. It is the biographer's spark of creation.

Even with that spark the life-writer's choices of method are formidable. There are writers who believe that they can wander around in their subject's life, put in scenes from different times, scramble sentences, and generally rummage at will. Leon Edel speaks their case: "The biographer may be as imaginative as he pleases—the more imaginative the better—in the way in which he brings together his materials. . . . He may shuttle backward and forward in a given life; he may seek to disengage scenes or utilize trivial incidents . . . to illuminate character; he has so saturated himself with his documents that he may cut himself free from their bondage without cutting himself free from their truth." To me this kind of freedom is license and takes the biographer into the realm of fiction. A writer has an obligation, I think, to be innovative and original in research but to be careful to do no violence to a subject's development—and consequently not to tamper with sequence. A writer, too, must guard against distorting a subject's passions, problems, or pleasures.

Above all, I believe, a biographer must not assume knowledge of a subject's future. Edel screams in agony: "When I pick up a biography, I know before I open the book that it is the life of a statesman. . . . Our point of departure in the reading of a biography is not necessarily in the cradle, but with the man who achieved greatness." I side with André Maurois, who thinks that Edel "wants us to play a rather curious game of make-believe." Paul Murray Kendall agrees that all readers engage in make-believe as they begin a biography—they know that Woodrow Wilson became president, but they do not usually worry about his future as they trace him through childhood and early career. We know that we are the sum of our experience; we expect to follow a written life as it grows. How else can a life be simulated? Artists really do not ignore logic—they may conceive a new logic, but they follow its boundaries. Biographers do not have the luxury of tinkering; their subject's life is their logic. Straying produces untruth.

Another pitfall the biographer must avoid is that of overidentification with a subject—superimposition, if you will, of the writer on the life being simulated. This is a real problem in modern life-writing, because life simulation involves reexperiencing the past with a subject. From this coexistence can come an almost unnoticed familiarity, a feeling that you—the writer—know your subject so well that you can predict reactions, feelings, jealousies—that you two think alike. Here the veil of existence seems nearly breached. How easy it would be to speak a subject's mind, and how specious! Years of acquaintance with your friends may lead you to a general sense of their feelings, but would you dare guess a friend's inner beliefs if they were never told to you? When your spouse enters the voting booth, are you absolutely sure?

How dare a biographer assume a thought, a bias, a prejudice of a subject unless some letter, some speech, some reliable source speaks? Freeman, who lived with General Lee for nearly twenty years, confessed that he never knew what was in Lee's mind unless he found the thought expressed somewhere. I lived with John Pershing for eighteen years and came to feel some friendship with him. I do not know to this day what his thoughts were—only what he said some of them were. To me the biographer's most forbidden ground is personal assumption. Of a subject's thoughts or beliefs nothing can be assumed.

I am not arguing that some things may not be taken as givens, that a writer may not use familiar things without racing for a footnote. All historians strive for verisimilitude, and one of the best ways to achieve it is to mix the sounds and sights of a place with action. This kind of art is at its best lost in its craft. Garrett Mattingly's classic *The Armada* is a good case study. He may assume, and use without fear of critic's horror, the sounds of the sea and ships, the sounds of wind and sail, the smells of powder and cordage. Freeman may loose the iron clangor of Gettysburg, the cries of charging, dying soldiers, for these are facts of his war. T. Harry Williams may rely on Louisiana's summer heat to shape one of Huey Long's harangues—and both writer and speaker show the impact of place. All these devices will be true to subject and circumstance—hence to art.

All other considerations aside, the biographer's goal is to evoke from the past the essence of a subject, the character that quickened blood and bone. It is the biographer's job to offer a subject to posterity—and that is no small responsibility. For that reason I think that the biographer's fundamental obligation is to understand—understand in all dimensions of the word.

For me, nothing is more necessary to the evocation of a life than full understanding of the person. More than that, I think that it is vital to understand a subject with sympathy and perhaps even to share viewpoints and ideas. I confess that this can be carried too far. Possibilities of oversympathizing hit me when I was working on my life of Stonewall Jackson. In the middle of a letter from General James Longstreet to Lee I struck a paragraph critical of Jackson and took it personally! That did seem to be a bit much. But in retrospect I was glad to realize that empathy had happened.

Similarly, when I became irritated with General Leonard Wood, I realized that part of me had reached some meeting ground with Pershing's prejudices. Lately I have started a Life of Field Marshal Douglas Haig, commander of the British armies in France during

64   World War I. He is controversial, engages hot enmity from many studies as the consummate butcher in a butcher's war. I began with that impression, but after some time in his company, I feel pressures and considerations that negate any label. Empathy is happening. I have glimmers of what I hope is understanding.

Understanding can come in various ways. Experience can aid the biographer in evaluating evidence. This idea came recently, as I thought about a life of Jefferson Davis that I would like to write someday. The book would be far different from the one I would have written four or five years ago. A tour of duty in university higher administration has given me new perspective on Davis as Confederate president. Crosscurrents of constituencies, administrative pressures, the iron grip of money—all are parts of Davis's life. I simply would not have appreciated them had I written earlier. I could not have achieved understanding, much less empathy.

Empathy is a quality, I believe, that gives biography an edge in attraction. A book that welds reader to subject commits a special kind of act: it offers a touch of friendship.

That touch is one of the reasons why biography is so much an agent of humanism. At its best, biography brings a touch of humanity from the past and can, if deftly done, offer a glimpse of humanity in microcosm.

There is an important connection between a biographer and a subject—the impact of one humanity on another. The good biographies really offer a special blend of two people, two humanities, a dual view of the human condition. Interestingly enough, both humanities focus on the same time, one as present, one as past, and provide almost stereoscopic perception.

As the biographer relives the past through the subject, so the subject evokes the past and serves the present. There is, in this unique relationship, part of the human continuum. "Never," says Jean Paul Richter, "does a man portray his own character more vividly, than in his manner of portraying another."

Times and things and thoughts change; ideas, fetishes, prejudices shift, but the interaction between biographer and subject still fascinates—and proves that one age can, through the art of biography, understand another, can touch and be understood—and hence can persist.

That persistence is the finest essence of humanism.

Five Catherine Drinker Bowen

The Biographer's Relationship with His Hero

"One should write only about what one loves." ("*On ne doit pas écrire que de ce qu'on aime.*") Renan, the biographer and historian, said it in the last century and for this writer at least it is profoundly true, the more impressive because in Renan's lifetime he withstood prolonged literary attacks. If so tough fibered an author confessed that he loved his subjects, why might not the rest of us do the same? For a considerable time it was unfashionable to admire one's biographical hero; the debunking period lasted a full generation. Lytton Strachey started it and on the whole it was a healthy movement, a reaction against the laudatory familial biography of the nineteenth century. But Strachey was a brilliantly talented writer; his imitators and followers had not his genius and the art of biography suffered. We outgrew the fashion, perhaps because debunking is easy and what is too easy does not hold up. Trollope said, "There is no way of writing well and also of writing easily." But the stigma remained; a book was not true unless it was malicious.

After the debunking era, biography went through no more literary fashions. Indeed, to the general surprise it has become immensely popular. One of the advantages of being a biographer is this freedom from changing literary modes. People want to read the authentic record of other people's lives and they do not want the story clothed in fashionable obscurity, imagery, symbolism. The modern biographer, if he chooses, can write as John Aubrey wrote two centuries ago in *Brief Lives*, or as Isaac Disraeli wrote in *The Literary Character*, or *The History of Men of Genius*—provided the modern writer is equally talented. He can use facts, dates, explanatory parentheses. He can proceed from point to point, from incident to incident with no apology for being old-fashioned, outmoded. Punctuation too is a matter of choice. The biographer can sprinkle the page with commas or, if his ear for rhythm is keen and his sentence structure is firm, he can arrange his punctuation as he pleases. Best of all, the biographer is not required to declare that life is a cruel and total absurdity, nor to follow his hero inevitably downhill to drugs, casual sex, and a drearily inconspicuous suicide.

This is not to imply that the biographer invariably approaches his work with love in his heart. There are many considerations besides love that may give the biographer his initial inspiration. I asked Miss Prescott in England why she chose Queen Mary Tudor to write about. No subject could be more difficult. In that ill-starred life tragedy followed tragedy; Mary's life was one long defeat. She loved her Spanish husband and was not beloved; she yearned for children to the point of imagining herself pregnant; her deepest instincts were denied outlet and she ended by earning in history the epithet of Bloody Mary. Miss Prescott looked me full in the eye and said, "I chose Mary Tudor because I thought she would make money for me."

One thinks of the traditional advice given the woman about to choose a husband: "Money first, love will follow." Surely it had been that way with Miss Prescott; a tragic story has not been more compassionately told. But it is indeed true that the biographer does not fall in love with his hero at first sight and remain infatuated. Love comes slowly, after deep acquaintance and many arguments back and forth, though one can judge this only by one's own experience. With Edward Coke, for instance, I had a struggle that could have ended in divorce. Here was a brave man, chosen to illustrate a historical point. But he was also stubborn, vain, disagreeable, and capable of cruelty. Contemporaries feared Mr. Attorney General; he earned widespread hatred for his bitter, relentless invective as prosecutor. At Ralegh's trial Coke behaved shamefully. Was this, one asked, the way our freedoms came to pass—in reverse as it were? Strange, that social progress can be achieved through an instrument so far from perfect! My workbook argued the point. "Coke was brutal beyond any excuse. Must I love him, must I even *like* him?" "No!" I wrote. "But I must be engaged with him, married to him, at one with him yet independent, rearing back to look at him."

In retrospect, it seems naïve; one forgets the deep involvement that comes with a five- or six-year book. As a definition of marriage proper, what the workbook said would not do. But as definition of biographical marriage it is valid enough. Perhaps what the biographer needs is not love so much as identification with the hero.

Whether or not one likes one's subject, it would be fatal to choose a hero with whom one could not identify. "Relate" is the current psychiatric phrase. A biographer can relate to the most diverse and seemingly unsympathetic characters. Something in the subject's life has touched the biographer's own experience, even though the deed came no closer than a wish.

Biographers approach their books at certain stressful periods in their lives. (The lives of artists are bound to be stressful, without stress they would feel themselves lapsing unconscious.) Tchaikovsky went through his days in a state of neurotic anxiety that at times bordered on madness. "Fear and I were born twins," said Thomas Hobbes, in one of the more surprising confessions of history. Perhaps fear, like neurotic anxiety, is to some natures a necessary stimulus. I think no one could write these lives who had not experienced neurotic fear, just as one could not write of Disraeli if he had not felt ambition, or of Balzac if he did not himself know the *furor scribendi.* "The need to express oneself in writing," said Maurois, "springs from a maladjustment to life, or from an inner conflict, which the adolescent (or the grown man) cannot resolve in action."

Maurois goes on to confess that he wrote his first biography, *Ariel: The Life of Shelley,* "because it was an expression of one of my conflicts. Shelley had come from a family from which he wanted to escape, and so did I. The problem of Shelley was also my problem. My personality was also expressed in *Disraeli.* He was Jewish. I was Jewish myself. He was for me an example of how to get on with a Christian society. Proust, Chateaubriand and Balzac I did because I admired them as writers. The choices were guided by my inner feelings, whether I can get on with this man or this woman. I couldn't accept the idea of spending three years of my life with someone I didn't like."

On the other hand the biographer is himself puzzled at how completely he can identify with diverse and seemingly unsympathetic characters. The surprise comes later, when he reads his published work. While he is writing he is too absorbed to be thinking about such things as identification. When the biographer has chosen his subject and sits down to read, what he is actually doing for the first three or four months is to make the acquaintance of his hero. Everything comes as grist to this mill: time, place, climate; the hero's friends, his enemies, his appetites physical and spiritual. Any least word about the hero's appearance, how he looked and dressed, is cherished as a lover cherishes the most fugitive news of his beloved.

68   There is a musical comedy song which perfectly expresses the biographer's condition at this stage. Sitting in the research library the tune goes through his head: "Getting to *know* you, / Getting to know all *about* you . . ."

Yet one can be deceived, at first reading and first study. It may indeed be years before biographer and hero come to terms; it is extraordinary how the material can lead astray. Theodor Reik, in his book, *Listening with the Third Ear,* has told how Lytton Strachey changed his mind about Queen Victoria while he was writing her biography:

> Studying the early life of the young Queen, [Strachey] did not like her very much. He saw her as a spoiled, overly self-assured and level-headed girl. He treated her at first with a certain ironical remoteness and with little sympathy. The more he studied her life and the more he began to understand her personality and the environment that helped form it the more sympathetic he became. At the end, when he speaks of the Queen in her last years, you feel genuine human warmth, appreciation, and admiration for an impressive personality. He started with little affection for his subject, and ended practically in love with the old lady.

With Sir Francis Bacon I had something of the same experience. I began his biography influenced by immediately previous years of reading for the life of Sir Edward Coke, who was Bacon's bitter rival both in the law courts and privately. Alexander Pope had called Bacon the wisest, brightest, meanest of mankind and I was inclined to agree. But when I began to study Bacon's works and his career more deeply I recognized my bias and saw that my hero's fall from high estate was no matter of smallness or meanness but tragedy in the grand manner, to be approached not with condemnation but with awe. In the end a biography that had begun in doubt finished on a note of solemn celebration.

A biographer's relationship with his hero can operate two ways. Sometimes the subject takes over, the author merely follows along. With Francis Bacon one was writing about genius. And when one does that, it is the genius that makes the rules. "In many instances," says Maurois, "it is a question whether the man we study was a really great man or a rather base character. The biographer has to choose. He cannot write a complete life of a man without deciding whether he likes him or not, whether he trusts him or not. Of course he may decide that, like most human beings, his hero was a mixture of greatness and weaknesses, but that also is an interpretation."

Even the biographical scene—the time and the place—can enlarge a writer's horizon. One has sat in the Long Parliament with Cromwell, or at the Constitutional Convention with Madison and Washington. One has walked the London streets in a plague year and has seen doors black-lettered in the houses of the sick: *Lord have mercy on us.*

Is all this to have no influence, leave no scar? Can the author put it from him only by writing *finis* to a book? Even dreams leave their residue; a day, a week can be colored by a fleeting picture seen in sleep. As to the effect a biographer's hero can have upon him, there is no way of overemphasizing it. To spend three years or five with a truly great man, reading what he said and wrote, observing him as he errs, stumbles, falls, and rises again; to watch his talent grow if he is an artist, his wisdom develop if he is a statesman—this cannot but seize upon a writer, one might almost say transform him. When the book is done the author returns to the outer world, but actually he will not be the same again. The ferment of genius, Holmes said, is quickly imparted, and when a man is great he makes others believe in greatness. By that token one's life is altered. One has climbed a hill, looked out and over, and the valley of one's own condition will be forever greener.

Six

Justin Kaplan

The "Real Life"

It is almost a commonplace now to speak of an ongoing "golden age of biography" that had its beginnings in the mid-eighteenth century. Since then the strategies, understandings, and supporting disciplines of biography have become more complex. Contemporary writers and critics occasionally acknowledge its speculative and crypto-fictive nature along with the existence of an old question: whether biography is a branch of history or a branch of literature, a work of record or an imaginative exercise. Some believe, as I do, that the biographer is essentially a storyteller and dramatist—Henri Troyat's superb *Tolstoy* is much to the point here—and that a strong case should be made for enlarging the term "literary biography" to include books that have literary qualities and not necessarily literary subjects.

But the stated aims of biography have remained remarkably consistent during two centuries and also consistently touched with a degree of presumption. "The business of a biographer," Samuel Johnson said, "is . . . to lead the thoughts into domestic privacies and display the minute details of daily life." Boswell's purpose was to enable mankind to see the subject "live, and to 'live o'er each scene' with him, as he actually advanced through the several stages of his life." Another familiar declaration, this one by Henry James, is more congenial to us in its terminology but not different in its fundamental emphasis on the flow of experience. "To live over people's lives is nothing unless we live over their perceptions, live over the growth, the change, the varying intensity of the same—since it was *by* these things they themselves lived."

We continue to expect biography to render not only the public and private events of a life but its intimate existential and perceptual textures, all adding up to the whole sense of a person. Freud and Jung on the one hand, Proust and Joyce on the other are among those who have provided models for the intricate and nuanced notation of interior states of being. And in the faith of a long "golden age" we tend to believe implicitly that biography *can* deliver the essential person and that there is a core personality, the "real Me," which we will find if only we dig deep and long enough. This belief, for the most part unexamined, is echoed in the well-meaning cant found in reviews—"the living and breathing presence," "larger than life," "the definitive account," and so on, evidences, incidentally, that the critical vocabulary of the golden age is still remarkably poverty stricken.

This extravagant faith in what biography can do has not been universal, of course, and there are distinct currents of reaction and skepticism about just how much biography can deliver even under the loose heading of "history," the documented existence of a real person. Reaction and skepticism have the effect of keeping biographers honest by making them write scared, conscious of what they may not be able to do and of what they do with the greatest difficulty. It appears that at best biography is only a plausible, inevitably idiosyncratic surmise and reconstruction, severely limited by historical materials that are loaded with duplicities and evasions. Even the great instrument of depth psychology, which once promised so much, turns out to be less essential than tact, empathy, empirical experience, and narrative flair.

We say of a successful biography that it is dramatically and psychologically coherent—it makes sense, it is believable, it is a good story. The writer starts off with a number of givens—birth and death, education, ambition, conflict, milieu, work, relationship, accident. He shapes them into a book that has the autonomous vitality of any work of the imagination and at the same time is "true to life" and true to history. In many respects biography is a feat of illusionism, sleight-of-hand, levitation; basic decisions and interpretations that appear to be the results of cautious deliberation are often made instantaneously in, and as part of, the act of writing; and for at least one moment each day the writer may feel like Mark Twain's titled charlatans putting on a performance of "The Royal Nonesuch." At other moments, proud as Ahab, his fixed purpose "laid with iron rails," the biographer may "strike through the mask" only to find, without nudging from Erving Goffman, that the pasteboard mask was what it was all about in the first place and that the work and the career—the public manifestation—may be more significant than the hidden self or selves. Isn't that, after all, one way we distinguish major lives from lesser lives, especially among writers? There may even be a principle in operation which determines that the size of a biography should be in inverse proportion to the size of the subject, as exemplified by Michael Holroyd's *Lytton Strachey* and Sybille Bedford's *Aldous Huxley*. (A notable exception is Geoffrey Scott's spare, elegant, and luminous *The Portrait of Zélide*.)

For all his dedication to interior states of being, Proust claimed that in the long run it was impossible, because of the nature of love, for one person to give an objective or even moderately reliable account of another, much less a "true" one. The nineteenth century was a time of burning archives, for the rise of intimate biographical inquiry and an avid reading public had added a new terror to death. This was the terror not only of having secrets unlocked and privacies violated but also of being misrepresented and misunderstood in a dull, bad book, in "those two fat volumes with which it is our custom to commemorate the dead," Strachey wrote. "Who does not know them with their ill-digested masses of material, their slipshod style, their tone of tedious panegyric, their lamentable lack of selection, of detachment, of design?" Recognizing the risks and adversary relationship inherent even in the best-disposed biographies, some writers turned to autobiography in self-defense. "The volume is a mere shield of protection in the grave," Henry Adams said when he presented a privately printed copy of his *Education* to Henry James. "I advise you to take your own life in the same way, in order to prevent biographers from taking it in theirs." Biographers had become murderers, and their subjects, fugitives.

Adams was a burner of papers; so was Henry James. Mark Twain claimed to be one but in fact kept a personal archive, parts of it still surfacing, that was nothing less than a monument to papyrophilia, an unreasonable attachment to anything made of paper. Together with a series of spellbinding but frequently unreliable oral reminiscences that had the effect of a smoke screen or the ink cloud of a squid, he made this archival material available to his appointed biographer, Albert Bigelow Paine, but he imposed severe restrictions. Mark Twain was skeptical about what biography could accomplish and he resented Paine's venture, even though he himself had encouraged it.

The little prefatory note Mark Twain wrote for his autobiography rationalizes this skepticism and resentment and also displays a somewhat uncharacteristic, nearly Proustian, concern with psychological continua:

> What a wee little part of a person's life are his acts and his words! His real life is led in his head, and is known to none but himself.

All day long, and every day, the mill of his brain is grinding, and his *thoughts*, not those other things, are his history. His acts and his words are merely the visible, thin crust of his world, with its scattered snow summits and its vacant wastes of water—and they are so trifling a part of his bulk! a mere skin enveloping it. The mass of him is hidden—it and its volcanic fires that toss and boil, and never rest, night nor day. These are his life, and they are not written, and cannot be written. Every day would make a whole book of eighty thousand words—three hundred and sixty-five books a year. Biographies are but the clothes and buttons of the man—the biography of the man himself cannot be written.

Mark Twain was thinking about precisely the kind of life behind life that by and large remains inaccessible to the biographer except through speculation, and he is derisive on the subject of speculative approaches even to evident matters like "the clothes and buttons of the man." He describes Shakespeare biography, for example, as "an Eiffel tower of artificialities rising sky-high from a very flat and very thin foundation of inconsequential facts," a fifty-seven-foot-high brontosaur that looks convincing enough in the natural history-museum but is made of six hundred barrels of plaster of paris and maybe only "nine old bones."

Wilfred Sheed once divided American writers into two classes, the hiders and the strippers, and in the popular understanding of their work and personality Mark Twain seems to belong with the hiders and Walt Whitman with the strippers. Like his friend and mighty contemporary Thomas Eakins, Whitman adored the naked truth in all its forms. But if Whitman, one of the fathers of confessional poetry, is indeed a stripper, he manages to make nakedness an ultimate disguise, and so he becomes an extraordinarily problematic subject for biography. This passage from "Song of Myself" may be the Whitman counterpart of Mark Twain's prefatory note:

> Trippers and askers surround me,
> People I meet, the effect upon me of my early life or the ward
>   and city I live in, or the nation,
> The latest dates, discoveries, inventions, societies, authors old
>   and new,
> My dinner, dress, associates, looks, compliments, dues,
> The real or fancied indifference of some man or woman I love,
> The sickness of one of my folks or of myself, or ill-doing or loss
>   or lack of money, or depressions or exaltations,

> Battles, the horrors of fratricidal war, the fever of doubtful
>   news, the fitful events;
> These come to me days and nights and go from me again,
> But they are not the Me myself.

He goes on to describe the "Me myself" standing "apart from the pulling and hauling," "both in and out of the game, and watching and wondering at it." What makes this passage especially suggestive is the probability that this "Me myself" is not the biographical Walt Whitman at all but a dramatic persona created for poetic purposes and also for the liberation of the biographical Whitman from some covert stage of development. He was both a stripper and a hider. Even when he says,

> Camerado! This is no book;
> Who touches this, touches a man,

he may mean that his book was all that he chose to show of himself.

The house on Mickle Street in Camden that Whitman occupied as an old man reminded at least one visitor, because of its disorder, of a field after a cornhusking, piled with shucks and stalks. From boxes and bundles in the store room, from a big iron-banded double-hasped trunk standing against the bedroom wall, Whitman released drifts and billows of paper, almost every imaginable variety of record—manuscripts, yellowed scraps of paper, notebooks and diaries, scrapbooks, letters received and drafts of letters sent, printers' proofs, photographs, clippings. This paper tide, which he stirred with the crook of his invalid's cane, covered the floor, churned around his feet, seeped into the corners of the room and under the furniture and was tracked out into the hallway.

Horace Traubel, a Camden neighbor who became, as he liked to think, Whitman's Boswell, found on the floor, among other things, the celebrated letter Emerson wrote in 1855 greeting the author of *Leaves of Grass* "at the beginning of a great career" and speculating that there must have been "a long foreground somewhere, for such a start." The floor also yielded up manuscript fragments and beginnings hinting that in this long foreground a great transformation had taken place along with the birth of an overriding purpose, to write his country's poems, to become, as Whitman said, "a master after my own kind."

Yet there were evidences that a less robust spirit had also been at work in the foreground, a spirit covert, hesitant, ashamed, and per-

turbed. "There is something in my nature *furtive,* like an old hen,"
Whitman said, adding that as a description of myself he was willing
to accept the word "artful." He said that there were "truths which it
is necessary to envelop or wrap up," that there was an "inexplicable
element of every highest poetic nature which causes it to cover up
and involve its real purpose and meaning in folded removes and far
recesses," to create personal myths and suppress personal history.
He was hardly even conscious of having consistently reshaped his
past to make it conform to an image of himself—ample, serene, and
masterful—which he arrived at long after the events concerned.
Whitman biography, like practically all biography, has to begin with
legend.

"Some day when you are ready and I am ready," he said to Traubel,
"I will tell you about one period in my life of which my friends know
nothing: not now—not tomorrow—but some day before long. I want
to tell you the whole story with figures and all the data so that you
will make no mistake about it." A week later he said, "You'll hear
that in due time—not tonight. That cat has too long a tail to start to
unravel at the end of an evening." He hated to be questioned, and
when pressed, no longer volunteering, he closed down into obstinate
silence, just as he locked his bedroom door each night. Traubel, as
hard as he tried, never managed to get him to tell the "whole story"
or even any fragment of it and began to suspect that perhaps there
was no story to tell. "There is a secret," Whitman insisted quietly.
"You will sometime see that there is a secret." The subject came up
again. "I want you to keep on asking till I answer," he said, "only not
tonight—not tonight." Biographers have kept on asking.

Despite his unique role as confidant and daily companion, Traubel
knew there were papers he could never be permitted to see as well as
stories he would never be permitted to hear. From time to time, as he
had been doing since he had his first paralytic stroke and thought he
was about to die, Whitman systematically sorted out and destroyed
parts of his archive. He explained to Traubel that there were certain
things "too sacred—too surely and only mine—to be perpetuated."
There were documents that he did not destroy but instead carefully
altered, disguising identities or transposing genders. By the time he
died there was scarcely a period in his life that had not been "revised" in one way or another; there were even years that had practically ceased to exist so far as intimate documentary evidence was
concerned.

Whitman's overflowing records, so accessible and careless, were

76   ultimately guarded and recalcitrant, like their owner. They are the materials of biography and also the materials of a fable of biography. "This is not so much of a mess as it looks," Whitman said, pointing to the papers on his floor and table. "You notice that I find most of the things I look for, and without much trouble. The disorder is more suspected than real."

Seven

Mark Schorer

The Burdens of Biography

Many of you know the anecdote about Samuel Johnson and James Boswell in which Boswell, with his obsessive concern for the accumulation of more and more details of Johnson's life and character, was questioning a third person about Johnson in Johnson's presence, when Johnson suddenly thundered at him, "You have but two subjects, yourself and me. I am sick of both."

Let this anecdote serve as my text, and in a more special way than the exasperated Dr. Johnson intended, namely, that biography itself has two subjects, and two subjects only—the figure whose life is being re-created, of course, and the mind that is re-creating it, the scrutinizing biographer no less than the object of his scrutiny. Let me use it, too, to suggest that the largest burdens of biography are twofold: one, of course, on the man who has undertaken the work, responsibilities much more subtle than may at first appear and conceivably so enervating that he may well be tempted to throw up his hands and shout, "I'm sick of it"; the other on the ghost of the man who is not to be permitted the decent obscurity of death and who, seeing how he is being made to live, might well, had he a voice, shout, "I am sick of both!" And let me use this anecdote finally as a kind of warning, even as a request for forgiveness of what may well seem to be an exercise in egocentricity that goes far beyond Boswellian vanity. For I must be personal if I am to speak on this subject at all.

I spent some years in research for a biography and some more years in writing what proved to be a rather large book. I had not intended to speak directly about that book or of my experience in writing it. I had hoped to speak generally on biography as an art. I had written a biography but I had never read much about the nature of biography or how to write it. In preparation—as I thought—I have read a half dozen books, or more, on this subject, and I regret to say that I learned very little. It is difficult, but not impossible, to set up a definition of the novel more precise than E. M. Forster's quotation from the Frenchman Chevalley that a novel is "a fiction in prose of a certain extent." It is even more difficult to define biography, so various is it, or to set up rules for its composition, although this has been attempted. I am forced, for this reason, chiefly to posing some questions and then to answering them as well as I can from my own experience.

A writer of fiction, turning to biography, discovers the difference immediately (later, he will discover the similarities as well); as a writer of fiction he was a free man; as a biographer, he is writing in chains, as it were. As a writer of fiction, he invented his subject, even when he modeled it on real events and real people, and was free to handle it as he pleased; as a biographer, he is given his subject and is obliged to stay rigorously with its facts. This is, of course, a burden, but often, one discovers, a burden that it is a pleasure to carry. For facts can be surprisingly friendly, and they have, not infrequently, an eloquence, even a kind of poetry, that may well go far beyond the inventions of imagination.

I had thought, as I came to the end of my biography, that I would next write a short novel—a novel about Sinclair Lewis, no less, in which I could do some telescoping and some embroidering which the limits of biography did not allow, and also in which, with the happy disguises of fiction, I could use some episodes that my at least rudimentary sense of the power of legal restraints had not allowed. I gave up that idea. Almost simultaneously with the publication of my biography, a novel about Sinclair Lewis was published. It provided a sharply drawn picture of some of Lewis's most striking characteristics, but in its invented elements—chiefly, its plot—it did not do so well. It is known that toward the end of his life Lewis enjoyed the company of a young actress as his mistress. She was a few years younger than the older of Lewis's two sons, and in real life Lewis would try to amuse her with the company of people of her own age, including this son. But when now and then he urged the young man to take her out for an evening, to dinner or to the films, he complained to his mother: "I don't want to take her out. She bores me." In the novel I have in mind, the aging novelist's son falls in love with the young woman, and when in the climax of the story the father discovers the affair his world at last crashes into total ruin. But the facts, while less melodramatic, were much more interesting, certainly more macabre. After the young woman left Lewis to marry a man of roughly her age, Lewis decided to go abroad; but he wanted a companion, and he invited a number of old friends and a number of near strangers to travel with him. All refused. Then he turned to the young woman's mother, a plain, inarticulate, simple New Jersey housewife, who accepted. And Lewis, with his extraordinary gift for self-deception, wrote back to his friends to say how graciously the Florentines were receiving her. "Donna Caterina," they called her, he said. But in the obituary columns of at least one Florentine newspaper, she was referred to as *una vecchia gouvernante*—an old governess. Here I am happy to be confined to the pathos of fact.

Let me give you another and a much briefer illustration of what I have called the friendliness of facts. Lewis died of what we would call a heart attack; but in the official records of the Roman hospital in which he died, the cause of his death is given in another terminology, presumably a commonplace in the vocabulary of Italian medicine: *paralisi cardiaca*. Could I possibly have invented it? Paralysis of the heart. This, in its metaphorical significance, I had long before discovered was the very theme of Lewis's life and a major theme of the whole book: his incapacity for love. Is this not poetry? and more than that, magnificently, poetic justice?

There is then, first of all, the body of fact about one's subject. These details, if one is a responsible biographer, one accumulates with all the hoarding assiduity of a Boswell, the most trivial along with the most striking. One *must* accumulate them all, or as many of them as can be retrieved from mouldering documents, for until one is in possession of them all, one does not know two important things: one, what the book is to be about; and two, what shape the book will have. It is probable, however, that about halfway through the process of accumulation one begins to have some sense of each of these matters, since the accumulation is not made according to chronology but in a hit or miss fashion as one picks up scrap after scrap at whatever point it is offered. (For my book, for example, my earliest extensive researches, because I happened to be living in Italy when I began, were with the end of the Lewis life.) Italy, except for some newspaper accounts, did not provide much by way of documents, but it contained the places where he lived—his Florentine house, his last, gave me more eloquent facts than scores of documents could have—and it contained besides a host of living witnesses.

When one is writing the life of a person only recently dead, living witnesses are, of course, an essential source of information. And one discovers all too soon the burden that such evidence entails. Sometimes I wished that I had ten years more, for in that time most of those people would have gone away and I would no longer be confused by their conflicting tales and would in fact be free to say what I wished about *them*. Quite as often I despaired when, just as I was about to get to an important informant, he *did* suddenly go away.

The first problem with living witnesses is simply human vanity. It is natural enough that anyone who knows that he is to appear in a book will wish to appear to the best advantage. Inevitably, then, he will do one of two things, or both, when he talks to the biographer: he will be exasperatingly reticent or he will dress up the circumstances. Then there are those who wish to be memorialized as having had a more important association with the subject than the facts will support. Fortunately, if one has enough living witnesses, one can generally check the accuracy of one against the testimony of another or of others. And often, of course, a letter, a scrap of entry in a diary or a journal, a casual item in a newspaper, a published reminiscence will turn up to provide the control for which one is looking. This is not to say, of course, that documents in themselves are to be trusted simply because they are documents, even of the most personal kind. Leon Edel, the biographer of Henry James, who has read some seven thousand letters by James, tells us of the analytical scouring he must do to get beyond the "mere twaddle of graciousness" to the trustworthy kernel, if it is there at all. And Sinclair Lewis, after he was famous but still writing his aged father faithful weekly letters, mainly from Europe, enjoined his young nephew, who read these letters with adolescent fascination, not to take them very seriously, that he wrote his father only what his father wanted to hear. So documents, too, must be checked against other documents, and back against that talk from personal witnesses that may or may not represent the truth.

A third kind of difficulty presented by living witnesses evidences itself immediately when one is dealing with a personality like Sinclair Lewis's—at once so extreme in gregariousness and so short in patience. The number of associates that resulted from the first quality proposed an almost endless round of interviews which I finally ended rather arbitrarily, but I am not thinking of that problem so much as I am of the hurt feelings that resulted from the second quality. Lewis was like Richard Savage in at least one item in Johnson's life of that unhappy man: "It was his peculiar happiness, that he scarcely ever found a stranger whom he did not leave a friend; but it must likewise be added that he had not often a friend long, without obliging him to become a stranger." Hurt feelings lingering, even festering over the years, do not make for highly reliable testimony. One tends to come away with only the anger, the rancor, the wound—and beyond a certain point, these are not of much use to the biographer.

A more serious difficulty with living witnesses is the simple fallibility of human memory. I have told this anecdote before, but let me tell it again, because the general principle involved has again been amusingly illustrated, for me, since the publication of my book. Biography, as Bernard de Voto wrote, "is not concerned with the *must* but only with the *did*." Yet one soon finds, when writing the life of a man who gained great public prominence, that in many minds certain things *must* have happened even if they *did* not. A prominent man is, in many ways, a mythological man.

If Sinclair Lewis became the most famous man ever to have grown up in Sauk Centre, Minnesota, his youth there must have held the evidence, even if it was only belatedly observed. Thus, one of my witnesses, a contemporary of my subject, told me how, in June of 1902, graduating from the Sauk Centre High School in a class of seven, Sinclair Lewis, that baffled, awkward boy of seventeen, gave a brilliant valedictory address on the subject of "The Westward March of Empire." The subject was appropriate enough to the time, but the address itself was not appropriate to the academic circumstances of Harry Lewis. In this detail, the documentary control was easy enough to come by: the local newspaper under the proper date, which summarized the famous address and demonstrated quite clearly that it had been delivered, not by my subject, but by my informant himself. There is touching humility in this anecdote, but I fear only a rudimentary sense of history. On his graduation from a high school with a class that had three places of honor open to it, Sinclair Lewis was, for a change, completely silent.

This curious experience came back to my mind a few months ago when I had a letter of congratulation from my high-school English teacher in my sophomore year in the Sauk City (Wisconsin) High School—named after the same Indian tribe, an almost interchangeable town with Sauk Centre, Minnesota, but, it happens, a different one. She was writing to congratulate me. She always knew that some day I would be famous. (Let me say quickly that this is only *her* view.) She supposed that I would not remember her (of course, I do;

did she not dismiss me from class for snickering about a word in *Macbeth* for which Sauk City preferred a euphemism?). She was always, she said, afraid of me, because she felt that I knew so much more about the subject than she did, and that I would expose her ignorance. I was the "brightest boy in the school."

Ha! My academic record in Sauk City is no doubt quite as available as was Sinclair Lewis's in Sauk Centre, but I have no wish to examine it. I know what it was—highly undistinguished. And so was all my academic work until I was well into graduate study. My undergraduate record, today, would not admit me to any self-respecting graduate school, certainly not that of Michigan, probably not that of Harvard, where, as gawky as Sinclair Lewis at Yale, I mysteriously went.

This is all parenthesis, but not, I hope to indicate before I finish, as gratuitously parenthetical as it may now appear. And it leads me to the next point that I would like to raise; who is the best biographer for a given subject?

Of all the living witnesses whom I approached, only four declined to be of help. Two of these were men who had known Lewis intimately and planned to write biographical memoirs of their own; naturally, they did not wish to share their material with me. A third was a man who had known Lewis during a very large part of his life, had been Lewis's editor for many years, but unfortunately, was also the editor of one of those first two men who planned to write his own Lewis biography; naturally, his interests were with that book, not with mine. The fourth was Lewis's last secretary, the man with whom Lewis was living at the time of his death, the man who, in the last years in Europe, managed his affairs. His refusal to see me, made on the telephone in Rome, remains a mystery to me; but I am grateful to him, for his refusal also enabled me to make something of a mystery of him. Since he would not see me, I had to depend upon the only available evidence for that association—hearsay. Much of it came from interesting sources—Bernard Berenson, for example, who declared to me, "I know a minor Central European adventurer when I see one." It is only in this part of the book, I believe, the very end, and only because of the lacuna which the obdurate ex-secretary provided, that my fictional impulses necessarily came into play. They made for a nice bit of implied melodrama and, I believe, for truth of its own kind as well. And for once I was freed of the vexatious business of trying to force an informant to be truthful!

Now it is possible that those two men who had known Lewis over a number of years, or even his editor, would have written better biographies than mine. Samuel Johnson would have thought so. The best biography, in his view, is written by the subject himself; in other words, the best biography is autobiography. Had Johnson had the interest to write his autobiography, it would, I suspect, have been brief and incisive and honest and masterly; but we can be certain that it would not have given us that full-bodied portrait that the patient drudgery of Boswell created in the great masterpiece of all English biography. In the degree to which it would have been shorter it would have been less true. Johnson was a man of unusual self-knowledge, but he was also a man of unusual reticence. Boswell's very naïveté gave him an advantage; so did his habit of garrulousness. And Johnson, we should remind ourselves, was an exceptional man, fearful of a number of things but never of contemplating his own nature. Most men are. Certainly my subject was. He wrote many autobiographical sketches, and all of them are inaccurate and untrustworthy, deliberate softenings of what was harsh, deliberate alterations of fact for the sake of entertainment, confusions of fact, obfuscations—all in need of correction. One of my informants has told me that, toward the end of his life, Lewis spent many hours, usually in drunken rages, dictating fragments of his autobiography to her, all later to be assembled in a book. I have not been permitted to see her notes, if they exist, and until I am, I shall permit myself to doubt that they exist. Nothing in Sinclair Lewis's writings suggests that he could have been his own biographer.

I shall have something to say presently about the uses to which a writer's own works can be put by his biographer. At this point I wish only to point out the hazards. With a writer such as Sinclair Lewis, so little inclined toward candor with himself, it would be fatal to take with any literalness those fictional passages of his that do seem to arise from his immediate experience. Like Richard Savage, to whom I shall come in a moment, Lewis had mistaken preconceptions about the simple life but no gift for living it, yet he always yearned for a wilderness excursion. When his brother finally made such a trip into Saskatchewan possible, it began, for Lewis, as a series of drunken adventures and ended as a number of days so acutely uncomfortable that he abandoned the trip before it was half over and headed back for civilization. When he came to use the experience in fiction—in a melodramatic novel called *Mantrap*—the figure who corresponds to Lewis is the heroic and vindicated city man in the wilderness, and the novel provided a suitable film script for the talents of Clara Bow. In *Dodsworth*, which has commonly been read as an account of the decay of Lewis's first marriage, nothing can be trusted but the *feelings* of the hero for his first wife, and his *feelings* for the woman who was to become his second. But feelings are not precisely biographical fact. Alcohol was a grave problem for Lewis, who on untold occasions suffered the horrors of hangover and the acute pangs of guilt that go with that condition; but he almost never wrote about these matters. In one foolish story he began to, but soon turned the truly reported details into the mechanics of a tricky plot directed toward the kind of "happy ending" that he himself was never to know. Never trust the author, said D. H. Lawrence. Trust the tale. Do not, he meant, believe the author when he lectures us; believe only the conduct of the narrative itself, and the resolution of its values. If we follow this sound advice with Sinclair Lewis, we arrive at one conclusion: self-deception.

After the subject himself, the best biographer was, Johnson thought, a close friend, a man who had seen his subject in the most intimate circumstances of his life over a long period, who knew the accents of his talk, who knew his physical habits, the way he walked, the way he behaved at table, the way he laughed, the degree to which he permitted his sorrows to show. Again, one can only wonder.

Johnson himself, when he came to write the life of his friend, Richard Savage, produced a work of art—he could not do less; but did he, in a strict sense, produce a proper biography of Richard Savage? Had he known Savage less intimately, might he not have paused to question Savage's own account of his birth and upbringing, found his friend not the innocent victim of monstrous abuses but an unsuccessful fraud, found his friend's supposed mother not the implausible fiend who has come down to us through the *Life*, but an indiscreet woman unsuccessfully put upon by a small villain? Recent scholarship suggests such miscalculations in Johnson's narrative, and so, indeed, does the narrative itself on any close inspection. Even Boswell, that glorious simpleton, had his doubts about this much of the narrative. And it is all the more surprising in that, at other points, Johnson could estimate his friend so ably. With what lovely irony he writes when he tells us how Savage's friends, eager to remove him from the threats of his debtors, arrange to ship him off to the wilds of

Wales. Savage, London born and bred, familiar only with the city, low life, and literature, had certain preconceptions about the country that Johnson was perfectly capable of defining and enjoying:

> He had planned out a scheme of life for the country, of which he had no knowledge but from pastorals and songs. He imagined that he should be transported to scenes of flowery felicity, like those which one poet has reflected to another; and had projected a perpetual round of innocent pleasures, of which he suspected no interruption from pride, or ignorance, or brutality.
>
> With these expectations he was so enchanted, that when he was once gently reproached by a friend for submitting to live upon a subscription, and advised rather by a resolute exertion of his abilities to support himself, he could not bear to debar himself from the happiness which was to be found in the calm of a cottage, or lose the opportunity of listening, without intermission, to the melody of the nightingale, which he believed was to be heard from every bramble, and which he did not fail to mention as a very important part of the happiness of a country life.

And yet, in spite of such perspicacity, the whole may very well be based on a miscalculation for the very reason that these men were intimates, had loved one another too much in life, too little, perhaps, in the imagination. There are deeper forms of intimacy than friendship.

Personal intimacy with one's subject would certainly have those advantages for the biographer that Johnson names, but does it not have certain disadvantages, too, and perhaps larger ones? Personal intimacy can readily lead to panegyric, which is not biography, for there are obligations to friendship even after one's friend is dead. Inversely, if hurt feelings are involved, it can lead to self-protective distortions and omissions, which are the chief faults of the first Mrs. Lewis's *roman à clef, Half a Loaf,* and her more recent biography of Lewis, *With Love from Gracie.* Personal intimacy, more significantly, may lead to mere memoir, which again is not proper biography, books of the "I Knew Him When" variety, or at least may permit intrusions of personal reminiscence which, if they do not decree the total shape, may yet throw the whole off balance (the only flaw in Andrew Turnbull's otherwise beautiful life of Scott Fitzgerald).

There is a further limitation: an intimate friend would almost certainly feel that he knew his subject to start with and conclude that much plain drudgery in accumulating all that detail, which a more impersonal biographer regards as essential to his enterprise, was not essential at all. For, believe me, the first thing that a biographer must be is a drudge. I wonder if either of those two men—one old and tired, the other a very busy and highly successful foreign correspondent— would, for example, have been willing to read through (and take the full notes which are routine for a trained scholar) Lewis's twenty-one novels, all but five of them of small literary worth and some of them almost unbelievably poor, let alone track down in any number of different libraries the hundred-odd stories, almost all of them worse than poor, which Lewis published in the highly paying but also highly ephemeral national periodicals of large circulation. I cannot believe it. And yet I do believe, with Professor Pottle, that among the obligations of a man who proposes to write a *literary* biography one of the first is to read through the complete works of his subject. And I will add a point that Professor Pottle does not, I think, make: that he will find that much of them he will have to read a second time, and some a third and a fourth.

And all this for extraliterary purposes, for reasons that have little to do with the literary worth of his subject's works. I do not mean to suggest that a literary biographer is not expected to deliver a literary judgment, indeed, a whole series of them; of course he is, that is his ultimate obligation. But even if the works are treated mainly as biographical events (as I chose, on the whole, to treat Lewis's) they must be read and analyzed, for in some important ways they are the clue to and even the chart of the mind and being of his subject. This is particularly the situation if the work is imaginative, and even if it is not generally autobiographical in the usual sense (and Lewis's certainly was not), it is nevertheless an autobiography of the spirit. Its lineaments are to be detected in the situations and themes that recur, in repeated and developing images, in certain character types that seem to haunt the author. Almost all of Sinclair Lewis's works, one discovers after a time, are built on the same general idea, of a character who is trying to escape from something restrictive into some kind of freedom. In the novels, the restrictions—convention, hypocrisy, injustice, institutions, et cetera—are metaphors, one finds at last, for a restriction that was unutterable for him in his life. For the second large theme of that life is Lewis's own frenetic and endless and impossible attempt to escape from the restrictions of his self into a freedom that does not exist.

We have gone beyond the drudge, who must accumulate, to the critic, who must analyze, and who is perceptive enough to see what is basically *there* in the work. The drudge alone could compile his material into a chronological catalogue, even a chronicle of sorts; but that is not proper biography. The critic alone, if he can see not only what is basically there in the work, but also how it threads its way through the whole mass of accumulated detail, will have moved toward the formal skeleton of a biography; but that is not yet proper biography either. No, now we need a third man, and you must forgive me for saying that he must be an artist, not only the man who can bring shape out of the mass but more especially the man who can give it living shape; and I do not mean only that he must make his subject live, but also that he must make him live in the reanimated history of his time, make him live in a living world. And now that we have come to the most interesting point, I too have reached the unutterable, the burden that is ineffable: I do not know how it is done. I can only hope that in some small way, perhaps, I did it.

We can talk about the shape if not about its animation. This brings us to the similarities with fiction, for biography, also, is a narrative art, and it seems probable that all the principles that pertain to fiction except for one—the free exercise of invention—pertain to proper biography. A novelist has his whole world of experience, real and imaginary, to draw from; how does he carve out of that limitless and undifferentiated mass the materials that fall into pattern in his beautiful, autonomous units? He has, of course, for each work, a theme, and his theme determines his selection of detail. The biographer finds his themes—the strains that seem most persistently to recur—in that mass of accumulated detail and selects from the mass accordingly. I am aware that some of my readers do not think that I selected drastically enough and others think that I did not select at all; the fact is that I did not, for example, report on every drunken rumpus, as one reviewer has complained, but only on, I suppose, some six or ten of them, whereas there must have been at least ten times ten and possibly one hundred times six of them. But if from my mention of six or ten, my exhausted reader has some sense of the exhausting intemperance to which Sinclair Lewis, in long stretches of his life, was addicted, I am at least partially vindicated: the reader, who carries the least burden, except perhaps on his pocketbook, has at least been made to suffer with my subject and with me. And while we are on intemperance and the problem of selection from the whole possible body of detail, may I remind you that it was only as recently as 1903, the year after Sinclair Lewis's inauspicious graduation from high school, that Sir Edmund Gosse arrived at the conclusion that the one horrendous fact about his subject which a biographer should under no circumstances reveal is his addiction to drink. If we were today to eliminate this phenomenon, what would the biographers of American writers have to write about?

For several centuries "the ethics of biography" (as Sir Edmund entitled his essay of 1903) was the subject of much discussion: what, in any body of accumulated detail, was clearly inadmissible by the biographer? Gibbon, in the eighteenth century, thought that everything was admissible, and so did Johnson except for one occasion when he reversed himself and opined that it was better to repress a detail than hurt the feelings of "a widow, a daughter, a brother, or a friend." In the nineteenth century, while biographies grew longer and longer, they tended to revert to their origins in England and become mere works of hagiography. Today, I believe, the problem of selection is not made more acute by what were once thought of as ethical considerations. One should write in anything that is true and relevant to one's themes—anything, that is, that will not bring us into court. In this sense, at least, therefore, the biographer today enjoys some of the freedom of the novelist, and he does not have to publish that famous and foolish disclaimer at the front of his book about how nothing in it has any relation whatever to any real person, now living or now dead.

Assume that our biographer has his several themes, those tensions or preoccupations or behavioral patterns that occur most frequently in the mass of the life, and that he can select his details accordingly. Like the novelist he faces a second step. All those themes must somehow be unified, the biographer, like the novelist, must find an appropriate emphasis, or general meaning. When I was about midway in my research, I decided that I would try to summarize Lewis's biography in a subtitle: *An American Life.* I had in mind at least a dozen things, not really separate but separable. I can mention a few. I saw Lewis's life, for instance, as representative of the curious social mobility of American life in general—the poor beginnings and the sudden, fantastic, uneasy success. I saw it more specifically as an

extreme example of the fate of so many American writers—the
quick supremacy and the long, dreary decline joined with an equally
dreary debauchery. I began to see Lewis's life as peculiarly American
in the very ambiguities that tore it apart—his love for his country,
sometimes nearly chauvinistic, and his unhappy dislike of much of
it. I might have borrowed a subtitle from Melville and called it
Sinclair Lewis: The Ambiguities. Or *The Paradoxes.* For the very
ambiguities of American life, those paradoxical polarities of an indi-
vidualistic society which destroys individuality, an affluent society
which does not permit millions of its citizens the merest decencies,
a peace-loving society which does best in a wartime economy—all
those ambiguities that engendered Lewis's ambiguous feelings about
his country are also represented in the profoundest ambiguities of
his own character. And now perhaps you can see how the biographer,
subjective being, enters the objective facts. For clearly I am talking
like a novelist, talking about America as it seems to me, and finding
in the objective materials of a single life facts that will support that
view.

We have, then, some themes and what is meant to be a unifying attitude. We must have, beyond these, a general shape, or form, or
rhythm—again, like the novel. Themes and attitude, taking always
into account the general chronology of real events which in large part
determined them, will in turn determine this. The shape of my book
seemed fairly obvious long before I was into it very deeply   a general
pattern of rise, climax, and frenzied fall, containing within it many
lesser patterns of rise-climax-fall, a few of them large. And like the
novelist, the biographer needs still another element; he needs a plot,
an element of persistent conflict that will animate not only the subject himself but that pattern which his life enacts, over and over in
little ways, and once and once only in the whole that it was. Here the
facts of Lewis's life were most obliging, and the central conflict
(highlighted, of course, by my own view of things) seemed clear
enough; first the quarrel of his environment with him, then his quarrel with his environment, and that quarrel turning very early but
with slowly increasing intensity into his quarrel with himself and
his attempt to escape it, to escape the self.

I begin to sound like an amateur psychologist and for that I am sorry,
since I tried very hard in my book to avoid precisely that. A biographer, like any other civilized man, should know about the develop-
ments of modern psychology, but I do not think that he should write

as if he were indeed a psychoanalyst. Some of my reviewers wished that I had; they wished that at some point I had said plainly, flatly, what was *wrong* with Sinclair Lewis. It was precisely because I was unwilling to make such a statement that I made the book so long. I wanted to give the reader all the evidence that I coherently could which would permit him to say to himself what was wrong with Sinclair Lewis. But more than that, I wanted him to believe that Sinclair Lewis was a living man, and I wanted him to be moved by his life. I do not think that the jargon of psychoanalysis would have heightened either the comedy or the pathos of that life. A friend of mine, a psychoanalyst, has recently sent me a paper of hers on a phenomenon that she has observed and calls "the Pollyanna Paranoid." This is the person who conceives of an impossibly beautiful future which, when it does not develop, as it cannot, permits him to feel betrayed and persecuted. The concept can explain a good deal about Sinclair Lewis, if not everything. But I insist that the term would hardly have improved my prose.

And this is the final matter that I must touch upon, and probably the most important. Thomas Carlyle, I believe, said that a well-written life is a much rarer thing than a well-spent one. I do not know if my life of Lewis is well written, but I do know that I gave as much thought as a novelist does to the kind of prose that would be most appropriate to that subject, to the tone that my prose would strike. Recently I was invited to attempt now a biography of Stephen Crane, and while I have still a good deal to learn about Crane's life (and hence of my relation to that subject) I know most of his writing, and already I am wondering what tone will be most appropriate to that subject. (I am thinking about something that I call to myself "*athletic* elegance.") But for the life of Sinclair Lewis, I decided, lived with so little dignity and so much fret and fury, and, on the literary side, producing so much loose and garrulous bulk, the tone must be casual—never exalted, seldom formal, but rather conversational, perhaps rambling a bit, frequently ironical, now and then a little snide. I wanted the reader to feel that I was talking to him, or as if he were overhearing me as I talked to Sinclair Lewis, saying in effect over and over, You did that . . . it was funny, wasn't it . . . how did it go again? . . . why?

It was only after I was well into the book, accustomed to that tone—or whatever tone it was that I achieved—that I began to wonder about my relationship to Sinclair Lewis and to begin to understand how much of that relationship was making the substance of the book. Not the facts; they were there. Not the themes; they were there. Not even the plot; that was there. But the general attitude, the whole coloration, because that was I, or rather, the two of us together. Here we can differentiate between what goes into fiction (*I*, really), and into history (*they*, really), and into biography (he *and* I). For is not biography, when we reduce it to its essential nature, simply—or complexly—the interpenetration of one mind by another, and is this not, for all the apparent objectivity one may achieve, a considerably subjective operation? "History," said the great Theodor Mommsen, "is neither written nor made without love or hate." He could have made that observation even more appropriately of biography. In my relationship with Lewis, as I began to scrutinize it and as it was revealing itself in my tone, there were both love and hate, and there were also pity, shame, much impatience. There were also self-love and self-hate and self-pity, and the shame and the impatience were as much for myself as for him.

Why did I—first of all—and now we are at what is really the beginning—why did I choose to write this life? It is true that I was invited to write it, but surely I could have said no. I believe now that from the outset I was challenged by what I unconsciously felt to be a strange affinity, an affinity perhaps only demonstrated by the fact that my literary tastes, as they matured, had moved about as far away from his as is possible. There was, of course, the obvious affinity of our beginnings—the same kind of raw small Midwestern towns, probably much the same kind of inept and unsuccessful boys in that particular man's world. But I discovered many more, and many that were more subtle. Should I try to spell them out now I would be writing my autobiography, or even confession, and I have no such inclination. But I can give you a hint or two: all the careless writing, all the ill-conceived ambitions, all the bad manners, all the irrational fits of temper, all the excesses of conduct, all the immature, lifelong frivolities and regrettable follies. That is a little of it. There is much more. And those of my critics who have complained of an imputed lack of sympathy with my subject might have said with equal accuracy and greater justice, with sharper perception certainly, and probably with more kindness, that I had refused to be self-indulgent.

Perhaps this is where the psychoanalyst is really needed—not in the biographer analyzing his subject, but beyond both of them, analyzing their symbiotic relationship. And it is perhaps this relationship that explains why one of those critics who complained of my want of sympathy—Mr. Irving Howe—found the book paradoxically moving, in spite of all my icy refusal to be moved.

Critics are not as wise as they sometimes sound and never as wise as they believe. I speak now as a critic, and a self-critic. My long conversation with Sinclair Lewis—my nine years captivity with him, one witty journalist called it—taught me a good deal. As I learned about him with all his stubborn deficiency in self-knowledge, I believe that I gained in self-knowledge. I am not a better man, certainly, for having written his life; but I think that I am a wiser one. And I can only hope that my gratitude to him for that will lighten a little the onus of the life with which I have burdened him.

Eight

Barbara W. Tuchman

Biography as a Prism of History

[handwritten: like the period in dayren]

Insofar as I have used biography in my work, it has been less for the sake of the individual subject than as a vehicle for exhibiting an age, as in the case of Coucy in *A Distant Mirror;* or a country and its state of mind, as in the case of Speaker Reed and Richard Strauss in *The Proud Tower;* or a historic situation, as in the case of *Stilwell and the American Experience in China.* You might say that this somewhat roundabout approach does not qualify me for the title of biographer and you would be right. I do not think of myself as a biographer; biography is just a form I have used once or twice to encapsulate history. *[handwritten: biography to capture a time period]*

I believe it to be a valid method for a number of reasons, not the least of which is that it has distinguished precedents. The National Portrait Gallery uses portraiture to exhibit history. Plutarch, the father of biography, used it for moral examples: to display the reward of duty performed, the traps of ambition, the fall of arrogance. His biographical facts and anecdotes, artistically arranged in *Parallel Lives,* were designed to delight and edify the reader while at the same time inculcating ethical principles. Every creative artist—among whom I include Plutarch and, if it is not too pretentious, myself— has the same two objects: to express his own vision and to communicate it to the reader, viewer, listener, or other consumer. (I should add that as regards the practice of history and biography, "creative" does not mean, as some think, to invent; it means to give the product artistic shape.)

A writer will normally wish to communicate in such a way as to please and interest, if not necessarily edify, the reader. I do not think of edifying because in our epoch we tend to shy away from moral overtones, and yet I suppose I believe, if you were to pin me down, that aesthetic pleasure in good writing or in any of the arts, and increased knowledge of human conduct, that is to say of history, both have the power to edify.

[handwritten margin note: comparison to portraits]

perception ↓

As a prism of history, biography attracts and holds the reader's interest in the larger subject. People are interested in other people, in the fortunes of the individual. If I seem to stress the reader's interest rather more than the pure urge of the writer, it is because, for me, the reader is the essential other half of the writer. Between them is an indissoluble connection. If it takes two to make love or war or tennis, it likewise takes two to complete the function of the written word. I never feel my writing is born or has an independent existence until it is read. It is like a cake whose only *raison d'être* is to be eaten. Ergo, first catch your reader.

offers narrow focus

Second, biography is useful because it encompasses the universal in the particular. It is a focus that allows both the writer to narrow his field to manageable dimensions and the reader to more easily comprehend the subject. Given too wide a scope, the central theme wanders, becomes diffuse, and loses shape. One does not try for the whole but for what is truthfully *representative*.

Coucy, as I began to take notice of him in my early research on the fourteenth century, offered more and more facets of the needed prism. From the time his mother died in the Black Death to his own marvelously appropriate death in the culminating fiasco of knighthood that closed the century, his life was as if designed for the historian. He suppressed the peasant revolt called the Jacquerie; he married the king of England's eldest daughter, acquiring a double allegiance of great historical interest; he freed his serfs in return for due payment (in a charter that survives); he campaigned three times in Italy, conveniently at Milan, Florence, and Genoa; he commanded an army of brigand mercenaries, the worst scourge of the age, in a vain venture in Switzerland, his only failure; he picked the right year to revisit England, 1376, the year of John Wycliffe's trial, the Good Parliament, and the deathbed of the Black Prince, at which he was present; he was escort for the emperor at all the stage plays, pageantry, and festivities during the imperial visit to Paris; he was chosen for his eloquence and tact to negotiate with the urban rebels of Paris in 1382, and at a truce parley with the English at which a member of the opposite team just happened to be Geoffrey Chaucer; he was agent or envoy to the pope, the duke of Brittany, and other difficult characters in delicate situations; he was a patron and friend of Froissart and owned the oldest surviving copy of the *Chronicle*; his castle was celebrated in a poem by Deschamps; he assisted at the literary competition for the *Cent Ballades*, of which his cousin, the Bastard of Coucy, was one of the authors; on the death of his father-in-law, King Edward, he returned his wife *and* the Order of the Garter to England; his daughter was "divorced at Rome by means of false witnesses" by her dissolute husband; he commanded an overseas expedition to Tunisia; he founded a monastery at Soissons; he testified at the canonization process of Pierre de Luxembourg; at age fifty he was challenged to a joust (in a letter that survives), by the earl of Nottingham, earl marshal of England, twenty-three years old, as the person most fitting to confer "honor, valor, chivalry and great renown" on a young knight (though, from what I can gather, Coucy was too busy to bother with him); he was of course in the king's company at the sensational mad scene when Charles VI went out of his mind, and at the macabre "dance of the savages" afterward; it was his physician who attended the king and who later ordered his own tomb effigy as a skeleton, the first of its kind in the cult of death; finally, as "the most experienced and skillful of all the knights of France," he was a leader of the last Crusade, and on the way to death met the only medieval experience so far missing from his record—an attested miracle. In short, he supplies leads to every subject—marriage and divorce, religion, insurrection, literature, Italy, England, war, politics, and a wonderful range of the most interesting people of his time, from pope to peasant. Among them, I may have rather reached for Catherine of Siena, but almost everyone else in the book actually at some point crossed paths with Coucy.

Once having decided upon him, the more I found out while pursuing his traces through the chronicles and genealogies, the more he offered. The study of his tempestuous dynasty dating back to the tenth century, with the adventures in law, war, and love of his ungovernable, not to say ferocious, forebears, made in itself a perfect prism of the earlier Middle Ages, which I needed for background. When I came upon the strange and marvelous ceremony of the *Rissoles* performed each year in the courtyard of Coucy-le-château, with its strands reaching back into a tangle of pagan, barbarian, feudal, and Christian sources, I knew that there in front of me was medieval society in microcosm and, as I wrote in the book, the many-layered elements of Western man. " layers "

As Coucy was a find, so for America at the turn of the twentieth century was Speaker Reed, or Czar Reed as he was called. As soon as I discovered this independent and uncompromising monument of a man, I knew I had what I wanted for the American chapter in *The Proud Tower*, a book about the forces at work in society in the last

96   years before 1914. He was so obviously "writable"—if I may invent
a word, which is against my principles—that I could not believe that,
except for a routine political biography published in 1914 and an un-
inspired academic study in 1930, nothing had been written about
him since his death in 1902. I now felt he was my personal property
and became seized by the fear that someone else would surely see his
possibilities and publish something in the years before my book—of
which he formed only one part in eight—could appear. Novelists,
I suppose, are free of this fear, but it haunts the rest of us from the
moment we have found an exciting and hitherto untreated subject.
Unbelievably, as it seemed to me, Reed remained invisible to others,
and as soon as I had written the chapter I took the precaution of arranging with *American Heritage* to publish it separately a year before the book as a whole was completed.

Reed was an ideal focus, not least because, as an anti-imperialist,
he represented the losers of that era in our history. Usually it is the
winners who capture the history books. We all know about Manifest
Destiny and McKinley and Teddy Roosevelt and Admiral Mahan,
but it is astonishing how much more dramatic an issue becomes if
the opponents'—in this case the anti-imperialists'—views are given
equal play and the contest is told as if the outcome were still in the
balance.

Though the events of the chapter are confined to less than a decade, I learned more about the ideas that formed our country than
I had in all my years since first grade. Reed led, through the anti-
imperialist cause, to Samuel Gompers, E. L. Godkin, Charles Eliot
Norton, William James, Charles William Eliot (and what a writable
character he was!), Carl Schurz, Andrew Carnegie, Moorfield Storey,
and to their attitudes and beliefs about America. All America's traditions were reflected there. Our development up to that time, and
indeed since, was caught in the prism of the struggle over expansion.

In form, the piece on Reed is a biographical sketch, which is a distinct form of its own with a long literary history. As a rule such
sketches are grouped in a collective volume, often by the dozen, like
eggs: *The Twelve Caesars, Twelve Against the Gods, Twelve Bad
Men,* and others. The advantage of the form is that one can extract
the essence—the charm or drama, the historical or philosophical or
other meaning—of the subject's life without having to follow him
through all the callow years, the wrong turnings, and the periods in
every life of no particular significance. Reed was an excellent choice

for many reasons: because of his outsize and memorable appearance—he was a physical giant, six foot three inches tall, weighing three hundred pounds, always dressed completely in black, with a huge clean-shaven face like a casaba melon; and, because of his quotable wit, his imposing character, his moral passion, and the tragic irony linking the two great contests of his life—one over the Silent Quorum and the other over the treaty assuming sovereignty over the Philippines. The first in its mad action was a writer's dream, and the second brought into focus the struggle of ideas at the turn of the century that marked the change from the old America to the new.

The Silent Quorum was a custom by which minority members of the House could defeat any legislation they did not like by refusing to answer "present" when called to establish a quorum for the vote. As Republican Speaker of the House, Reed had made up his mind to end once and for all the device that made a mockery of the congressional process. He succeeded in scenes, as a reporter wrote, "of such wild excitement, burning indignation, scathing denunciation and really dangerous conditions" as had never before been witnessed on the floor. Pandemonium reigned, the Democrats foamed with rage, a hundred of them were on their feet at once howling for recognition. One representative, a diminutive former Confederate cavalry general, unable to reach the front because of the crowded aisles, came down from the rear, "leaping from desk to desk as an ibex leaps from crag to crag." The only Democrat not on his feet at this point was a huge representative from Texas who sat in his seat significantly whetting a bowie knife on his boot.

Recalling that scene here is for me simply self-indulgence: I had such fun writing it. In the end, after five days of furious battle, Reed triumphed and succeeded in imposing a new set of voting rules that ensured that the will of the majority would thereafter govern. It was a long stride, as he said, in the direction of responsible government. Five years later, when it came to a vote on the annexation of Hawaii, and subsequently, on the treaty taking over the Philippines (which Reed as an anti-imperialist bitterly opposed), the purpose of the Quorum battle came to a test with inescapable moral fate, against himself. Still Speaker, he might—by summoning all his authority and manipulating every parliamentary wile of which he was the master—have stifled the vote, but if he did he would nullify the reform he had earlier won. He had to choose between his hatred of foreign conquest and his own rules. Knowing too well the value of

98   what he had accomplished, he could make only one choice. His victory over the Silent Quorum gave the victory to the expansionist sentiment he despised.

To me it seemed a drama of classic shape and I have always thought it would make a good play if only some perceptive playwright would come forward to write it. None has, I suspect because the playwrights of our era prefer to find tragedy in the lives of little people, in pale Laura and her glass menagerie, in the death of a salesman, in loneliness crying for little Sheba to come back. Something about our time does not like the great—though doubtless pathos and frustration are as true for humanity as the theme of *The Trojan Women*.

Another find for *The Proud Tower* was Richard Strauss, who served as a prism for a view of Imperial Germany on the eve of 1914. I did not want to do the usual portrayal of Wilhelmine Germany in terms of Wilhelm II and the militarists and the Agadir Crisis and all that. The business of rewriting what is already well known holds no charm for me. I would find no stimulus to write unless I were learning something new and telling the reader something new, in content or in form. I have never understood how the English manage to interest themselves in turning out all those lives of Queen Victoria, Wellington, Cromwell, Mary Queen of Scots—the large and the hackneyed. For the writer, plowing through the material for such a book must be like sitting down every day to a meal of Cream of Wheat: no surprises.

The choice of Strauss, which meant writing familiarly of music, of which I have no special knowledge, seemed almost too challenging. The reason for it was that, since I knew myself to be frankly prejudiced against Germans, I thought that both for me and the reader it would be fresh and interesting to approach them through the best they had to offer rather than the worst; through the arts, rather than through militarism, and through the one art in which they excelled—music. The result was that I enjoyed myself. Strauss proved satisfactorily Teutonic, and his wife, with her fanatic housekeeping and screams of wrath, even more so. Like Coucy, Strauss led everywhere: through his *Zarathustra* to Nietzsche, a key to the period; through his *Salome* to *fin-de-siècle* decadence; through conductorship of the Berlin Opera to Berlin and the beer gardens and German society and the Sieges Allee with its glittering marble rows of helmeted Hohenzollerns in triumphant attitudes; to Wilhelm II in

his fancy as "an art-loving prince"; to Vienna through Strauss's col-
laborator Von Hofmannsthal; to the brilliant explosion, as the new
century opened, of Diaghilev's Russian Ballet, of the Fauves led by
Matisse, the dance of Isadora Duncan, the sculpture of Rodin, the
Rite of Spring of Stravinsky, the scandal of Nijinsky's performance
as Debussy's Faun, and to all the frenzy and fecundity of that feverish
eleventh hour that was seeking to express itself in emotion and art.
I did not have to labor Strauss to carry out the theme; it was all in
Romain Rolland's uncanny prophecy after hearing Strauss conduct
Zarathustra: "Aha! Germany as the All-Powerful will not keep her
balance for long. Nietzsche, Strauss, the Kaiser—Neroism is in the
air!" Equally perceptive, the Austrian critic Hermann Bahr heard
in Strauss's *Elektra* "a pride born of limitless power," a defiance
of order "lured back toward chaos." Thus is biography welded to
history.

The life of "Vinegar Joe" Stilwell was the nearest I have come to
a formal biography although I conceived of it from the start as
a vehicle to carry the larger subject of the American experience in
China. Stilwell was not a lucky find like Coucy; he was the natural
and obvious choice. His career had been connected with China
throughout the period of the modern Sino-American relationship
from 1911, the year of the Chinese Revolution, to the penultimate
year of World War II, when he was the commanding American in the
China Theater. He represented, as I believe, the best that America
has tried to do in Asia, and he was in himself a representative American, yet sufficiently nontypical to be a distinct and memorable
individual. The peculiar thing about him is that he left a different
impression on different readers; some came away from the book ad-
miring and others rather disliking him, which only proves what
every writer knows: that a certain number of readers will always find
in one's book not what one has written, but what they bring to it.

Or it may be that I failed with Stilwell to achieve a firm characterization, which may reflect a certain ambivalence. I certainly admired him, and critics have said that I was, indeed, too energetically
his champion. Yet I was never sure that I would have actually liked
him in real life, or that he, to put it mildly, would have approved of
me. Perhaps it is fortunate that, although I passed through Peking in
1935 when he was there as military attaché, we never met.

This raises the question: Who is the ideal biographer? One who
has known his subject or one who has not? Boswell, I suppose, is

generally credited with the most perfect biography ever written (or, rather, personal memoir, for it was not really a biography), and the other biographies that stand out over the ages are mostly those written by friends, relatives, or colleagues of the subject: Joinville's *Memoirs of Saint Louis;* Comines' *Memoirs of Louis XI;* the three monuments by sons-in-law—Tacitus's *Life of Agricola,* William Roper's *Sir Thomas More,* John Lockhart's *Life of Sir Walter Scott;* Lincoln by his two secretaries, John Nicolay and John Hay; Gladstone by his colleague Lord Morley.

Such biographers have a unique intimacy, and if in addition they are reasonably honest and perceptive, they can construct a life that those of us not acquainted with, or not contemporary with, our subject can never match. If the contemporary biographer is blessed with Boswell's genius as reporter and writer, the result may be supreme. On the other hand, he may distort, consciously or unconsciously, through access to too much information, and produce a warehouse instead of a portrait. Lockhart's work fills four thousand pages in nine volumes; Nicolay and Hay's about the same in ten volumes. Unfortunately, in the matter of superabundance, the secondary biographer of today is not far behind.

The most immediate life is, of course, autobiography or diaries, letters and autobiographical memoirs. These are the primary stuff of history: the *Confessions* of St. Augustine and of Jean Jacques Rousseau; Pepys's *Diary;* Ben Franklin's *Autobiography;* the *Memoirs* of Saint-Simon; the letters of the Marquise de Sévigné; the journals of John Evelyn, Charles Greville, and the Goncourt brothers; the *Apologia* of Cardinal Newman; and, I suppose I must add, that acme of self-conscious enterprise, the *Education of Henry Adams.* Even when tendentious or lying, these works are invaluable, but they are in a different category than biography in the sense that concerns us here.

When one tries to think of who the great secondary biographers are, no peaks stand out like the primaries. There are, of course, the four gospels of Matthew, Mark, Luke, and John, who closely followed but were not acquainted with their subject. Although they tell us what we know of the life of Jesus, their motive was not so much biographical as propagandistic—a spreading of the gospel (which means good news) that the Messiah had come. Since then one may pick one's own choice: Carlyle's *Cromwell,* perhaps, Amy Kelly's *Eleanor of Aquitaine,* Sam Morison's *Christopher Columbus,* Cecil Woodham-Smith's *Florence Nightingale,* Leon Edel's *Henry James,*

Justin Kaplan's *Mark Twain* and *Steffens*. With apologies to them, however, I think the primary biographers still have the edge.

I shall never be among them because it seems to me that the historian—whether or not the biographer—needs distance. It has once or twice been proposed to me that I write a biography of my grandfather, Henry Morgenthau, Sr., a man of great charm and accomplishment, but though I loved and revered him, I shrink from the very idea. Love and reverence are not the proper mood for a historian. I have written one short piece on a particular aspect of his life, but I could never do more. *relationship between writer + subject*

In the subjects I have used I am not personally involved. The nearest I came was in the course of working on the Stilwell papers, then housed in Mrs. Stilwell's home in Carmel, when I became friendly with members of the family, who were, and are, very nice people and, I am happy to say, have remained my friends even *after* publication. Friendly relations, I have to acknowledge, inevitably exerted a certain unspoken restraint on writing anything nasty about the deceased general, had I been so inclined. However, I cannot think of anything I really toned down, except possibly the foul language to be found in Stilwell's diary. *must stay neutral* Restraint in that case, however, was less concerned with the family's sensibilities than with my own. Not having been brought up with four-letter words and explicit scatological images, I found it impossible to bring myself to repeat them, and yet to omit what I then took to be an indication of character violated my conscience as a historian. I eventually worked around that problem by a generalized, if nonspecific, reference to Stilwell's vocabulary. Exposed as we have all been since to the polite and delicate language of the last decade, I think now that I took the problem too seriously. I had no idea then how common and banal these words were in male conversation. *all in ones perspective*

More difficult was Stilwell's horrid reference to Roosevelt as "Rubberlegs," which truly shocked me. That he was a normal Roosevelt-hater of the kind in Peter Arno's famous cartoon, "Let's go to the Trans-Lux and hiss Roosevelt," and that he had a talent for inventing wicked nicknames, I knew, but to make fun of a physical infirmity seemed to me unforgivable. In a real agony over whether to include this usage or not, I conducted considerable research among people of Stilwell's vintage into the phenomenon of Roosevelt-hating, and even found an entire book on the subject. It showed that, compared to many things said in those circles, Stilwell's usage was run-of-the-mill, so I put it in, though it felt like picking up a cockroach. Though minor, this episode shows how a biographer can become emotionally involved with her subject.

Whether in biography or straight history, the writer's object is—or should be—to hold the reader's attention. Scheherazade only survived because she managed to keep the sultan absorbed in her tales and wondering what would happen next. While I am not under quite such exigent pressure, I nevertheless want the reader to turn the page and keep on turning to the end. This is accomplished only when the narrative moves steadily ahead, not when it comes to a weary standstill, overloaded with every item uncovered in the research whether significant or not. *must make decisions*

Unhappily, biography has lately been overtaken by a school that has abandoned the selective in favor of the all-inclusive. I think this development is part of the anti-excellence spirit of our time that insists on the equality of everything and is thus reduced to the theory that all facts are of equal value and that the biographer or historian should not presume to exercise judgment. To that I can only say, if he cannot exercise judgment, he should not be in the business. A portraitist does not achieve a likeness by giving sleeve buttons and shoelaces equal value to mouth and eyes. *metaphor*

Today in biography we are presented with the subject's life reconstructed day by day from birth to death, including every new dress or pair of pants, every juvenile poem, every journey, every letter, every loan, every accepted or rejected invitation, every telephone message, every drink at every bar. Lytton Strachey, the father of modern biography at its most readable, if not most reliable, and an artist to the last pen-stroke, would have been horrified to find himself today the subject of one of these laundry-list biographies in two very large volumes. His own motto was "The exclusion of everything that is redundant and nothing that is significant." If that advice is now ignored, Strachey's influence on psychological interpretation, on the other hand, has been followed to excess. In pre-Strachey biographies the inner life, like the two-thirds of an iceberg that is underwater, went largely unseen and uninvestigated. Since Strachey, and of course since Freud, the hidden secrets, especially if they are shady, are the biographer's goal and the reader's delight. It is argued—though I am not sure on what ground—that the public has a right to know the underside, and the biographer busies himself in penetrating private crannies and uncovering the failures and delinquencies his subject strove to conceal. Where once biography was devoted to setting up marble statues, it is now devoted, in André Maurois's words, to "pulling dead lions by the beard."

Having a strong instinctive sense of privacy myself, I feel no great obligation to pry into a subject's private life and reveal—unless it is clearly relevant—what he would have wanted to keep private. "What business has the public to know of Byron's wildnesses?" asked Tennyson. "He has given them fine work and they ought to be satisfied." Tennyson had a point. Do we really have to know of some famous person that he wet his pants at age six and practiced oral sex at sixty? I suppose it is quite possible that Shakespeare might have indulged in one or both of these habits. If evidence to that effect were suddenly to be found today, what then would be the truth of Shakespeare—the new finding or *King Lear*? Would the plays interest us more because we had knowledge of the author's excretory or amatory digressions?

No doubt many would unhesitatingly answer yes to that question. It seems to me, however, that insofar as biography is used to illumine history, voyeurism has no place. Happily, in the case of the greatest English writer, we know and are likely to know close to nothing about his private life. I like this vacuum, this miracle, this great floating monument of work that has no explanation at all.

Nine

Reassembling the Dust

"I know of no critics in modern times," Leon Edel, the biographer of Henry James, has reminded us, "who have chosen to deal with biography as one deals with poetry or the novel. The critics fall into the easy trap of writing pieces about the life that was lived, when their business is to discuss how the life was told." From scanning the reviews which greeted (in one form or another) my own biography of William Carlos Williams, I know the truth of Edel's statement. And I mention it because it is a curious phenomenon and, in an age which prides itself on the attention it has given to the critical act, a phenomenon which I find puzzling and hard to explain. It is as though, in the case of biography, the reader somehow believed that the life the biographer has assembled for us existed prior to the writing itself. I am only half playing when I say this, because it is axiomatic that the biographer must always be true to the facts—the literary remains—which he or she keeps finding, trying to make sense of it all in something like a final ordering.

But it is the other half of the problem which I want to look at: the biographer as creator, the dustman reassembling the dust, like the God of Genesis breathing life into a few handfuls of ashes. For the biographer is as much the inventor, the maker, as the poet or the novelist when it comes to creating a life out of the *prima materia* we call words, the very stuff, for example, that I am directing at you this moment. Is it not, after all, the *illusion* of a life which the biographer gives in the process of writing biography, something carried on perhaps over many years, a process of reassembling tapes and letters, discarded drafts and manuscripts, directives and memos, testaments and check stubs, the feel of names and places revisited, people known perhaps still among the living, words, words transcribed, written, uttered, words, words, and more words, which the biographer must shape and select and reorder, until a figure begins again to live in our imagination? It is extraordinary what the biographer feels when, finally, after writing and rewriting chapter after chapter of a person's life, after having lived for so long with the pale voices of the dead and perhaps with the still-insistent voices of the living who think that they were there, to suddenly feel something like light come streaming into the head, and to feel then the dust of all those words we call "facts" begin to take form, like the shape of the rose (to borrow an image from Ezra Pound) emerging out of the steel-dust particles when a magnet has been placed beneath their surface.

I remember how this moment occurred for me, and I keep learning that something like my own experience has been frequent with other biographers as well. Even after eight years of research, I was still finding Williams's letters in new archives or in private collections (a process, incidentally, which continues and which is bound to continue for some time). By then I had already collected thousands of such letters and was beginning to find a certain repetitiveness in the process. I decided at that point to play a game with the new packets of material which crossed my desk and, after looking at the date of a letter, try to guess what the general contents of that letter would be. I soon found that I could guess fairly accurately a good portion of the contents. It was like a tape going over in my mind: this was how Williams would have spoken to Pound at this point, this is how he would have addressed Louis Zukofsky or Allen Ginsberg or Denise Levertov or Robert Lowell. In a sense, then, the biographer had finally managed to become his subject. Other biographers have taken to wearing their subject's clothes or hat or shoes, others find their smoking habits and diets and tastes subtly or not so subtly changing to conform to their subjects', some have even gone so far as to interject themselves on the domestic scenes of their subjects, sometimes with an aggrandizement bordering on the violent, sometimes with something approaching filial piety. You can't live another person's words day in and day out without running up against some such occupational benefits or occupational risks. Those risks will differ of course for each subject, and several good novelists from Henry James on have used the biographer as their protagonist. Most of these novels have been in the tradition of the comedy of manners, though from the biographer's own standpoint I suppose the genre most apt would be the Romantic Quest. And at the heart of the romantic quest, remember, is the moment of the Grail, the visionary moment, the moment of the breakthrough.

Let us call this moment of breakthrough the *illusion* of the saturation point. I stress the word *illusion* because any biographer worthy of the name wants to ingest everything available on his or her subject and the truth is that more dust—new letters, new manuscripts, new memoirs by others who remained silent while you were doing your own work or who were spurred into writing perhaps because of your work—whatever, but more dust—has a way of collecting after your own work, you thought, was done. Such a state of things, this new stirring of the dust, is to be expected and even welcomed, for it shows a continuing or at least renewed interest in a subject that one already had found worthwhile exploring. Call this renewal of interest a kind of second life springing from the first life of the biography.

The only thing which might really trouble the biographer would be, I think, to discover that not only had the dust been stirred again but that something like a new rose pattern radically reshaping the life the biographer had already shaped had been part of the stirring. To watch all the dust reassemble again in a new configuration, and one which seemed to suit the dust more fully. Harold Bloom speaks of the anxiety of the later poet coming into the presence of the father's text. But that is as nothing to Ptolemy's meeting up with a Galileo, the son who would rearrange the sense of the world according to his own discoveries and his own imagination. For is not the biographer's primal desire the desire to father his subject, so that the "world" (i.e., one's interested readers) is satisfied with the illusion the biographer has given it and which can then pass for what one thinks of when one thinks of Subject X? How many of us think of James Joyce without thinking of Richard Ellmann's Joyce, or think of Hart Crane without thinking of Horton or perhaps Unterecker, or of Henry James without thinking of Edel's composite of a life?

How then does the biographer go about accomplishing this rich illusion of a life, this essential fiction? First of all, of course, not all biographers are sufficiently concerned with the shape of their fictions. In this they are like certain novelists in the American realist tradition who want the story without really giving all that much concern to formal considerations. There are those biographers who try to do the impossible by trying to get everything between the covers of two or five or nine volumes, in that attempt (frustrated from the start) emptying the dust bin over the grave of the dead as a memorial so that the dust sifts down and down in the shape of a pyramid, out of which monument the reader is then invited to make his or her own judgment, i.e., one's own private portrait. This gesture of omnipresence and omnipotence on the part of the biographer is perhaps that writer's last infirmity, and many have, finally, wearily, succumbed to that temptation. This is not to make an oblique strike at the long biography, for there is often good reason to publish a book or indeed several books which may exceed even the thousand-page mark. Besides, having perpetrated a long biography myself, I suppose I would like to defend my own actions as well. But Williams died just short of eighty and up to almost the very end he was in the midst of one or another of those American vortices which, like their natural cousin, the hurricane, have a way of forming and splitting up with unseemly haste. I still believe, however, that eight hundred pages devoted to Keats or to the two Cranes, all figures who died young, will appear excessive to any but the most devoted follower. On the other hand, Edel's five volumes on James, R. W. B. Lewis's biography of Edith Wharton, and Ellmann's life of Joyce, each certainly sustained meditations, seem to be appropriate in part because of the creative longevity of each of those figures.

Sometimes a case has to be made for presenting a particular life in detail even as one is in the act of re-creating the life, and that strategy likewise takes time. No one would blink twice if another long life were to appear which dealt with Faulkner or Pound or Eliot or Frost (though it is interesting that Lawrance Thompson's three-volume life should already have contracted to a single volume). But what about Williams? Did he really deserve a long biography? To listen to one camp of critics: no. To listen to another: yes, and it was about time. For part of a biographer's art will have to deal with the question of scope, of size. To do a mural or a cameo or a portrait? You don't just write a long biography by chance, and you will certainly not get it past a trade editor without making a very good case for the length of that life study. For myself, I was so frustrated by hearing the same myths about Williams—that he was incapable of serious, consecutive thought, that there was no real drama in the life of this New Jersey poet-doctor from a one-horse town, that *Paterson* and Williams's other poems were mostly precompositions, sketches for poems rather than poems, frenetically dashed off between delivering one baby and another—that I was determined to do what I could to set the record straight. With very few exceptions no one who had worked in any way with Williams's life and written of it had given the reader anything like a sufficient sense of just how complex and multileveled that life had been. Nor had anyone yet shown how intimately Williams had touched the imaginative lives of three gen-

erations of American writers. Profoundly touched by my own en-
counter with Williams, I wanted to do what I could as life-writer to
see at least that Williams was not dismissed now that something
like a full picture of the man in his time could be presented. The
story is there now, at least in place, and dismissal will have to come,
if it comes, either out of gross literary incompetency, indifference, or
malice. When I was younger it was Richard Ellmann's biographical
example in dealing with Joyce which had held me, and I see now that
what I wanted to give American audiences in particular was a book
about Williams peopled with his friends and enemies which would
be a counterpart in every way except in tone to what Ellmann had
offered in his homage to Joyce. I make no secrets about it. Call
it hubris, but my book would be a way of paying homage to the
father, of doing for Modern American Poetry what Ellmann had done
for European Modernism. There would be shortcomings of course.
There would be little on Frost or Sandburg or Robinson, and less than
I would have liked on Stevens or H.D. or even Marianne Moore. But
that would be because Williams had touched these lives only periph-
erally, if at all. In spite of which he would be my candidate for one of
the truly major American voices of our century, and here between
the covers of this book would be my case.

II

Looking back at what he had achieved in several biographies
on late medieval princes and statesmen, Paul Murray Kendall once
wrote that the biographer has the nearly impossible task of grafting
stone to rainbow. What he meant by this happy phrase was that the
biographer must take the unrecalcitrant facts as they appear to exist—in memoirs, diaries, journals, the rest of it—and so possess this
material as to create out of it the rainbow, the living simulation in
words of a life from all that we can discover about that person. In the
last poem he ever wrote, Hopkins spoke eloquently of this moment
of inspiration, the moment of the rainbow, and of that moment's
ability to keep *in*-forming its recipient, no matter how long it took
the poem to come finally to term:

> The fine delight that fathers thought; the strong
> Spur, live and lancing like a blowpipe flame,
> Breathes once and, quenched faster than it came,
> Leaves yet the mind a mother of immortal song.

Nine months she then, nay years, nine years she long
Within her wears, bears, cares and combs the same:
The widow of an insight lost she lives, with aim
Now known and hand at work now never wrong.

The biographer is both like and unlike the poet. He or she also feels
the same strong spur as the poet. But once the biographer has felt that
fine delight, that moment of light streaming into the head, the moment of the rainbow, there is still the forbidding pyramid of dust to
work with. The biographer may have caught something like the inner life of his subject, but how in heaven's name, after all, shall he go
about taking all those index card entries and all of those interviews
done on tape or in shorthand or by telephone and, in the case of the
subject as writer, analyzing or at least accounting for all those marvelous poems and essays, those memoirs and letters and libretti, and
transforming all into a readable narrative which shall do justice to
the subject? What tone shall he or she take toward the material, what
distance assume in relation to the subject, what language employ?
What strategies shall the biographer use by which to reassemble the
dust and reveal the pattern the biographer believes is somewhere in
the midst of all of that?

Biographers seem to have worked, at least until quite recently,
pretty much alone. First of all, they still come from widely divergent
disciplines. There is, for example, the field sociologist, the journalist, the historian, the psychoanalyst, the feminist, the Marxist, the
theologian, the professor of literature, even the professional biographer. Each comes to biography with different attitudes about the
field, different presuppositions, different purposes. In spite of which,
it seems to me, we must still learn how to tell a good story if we are to
tap the peculiar energies of the biography.

And how are we to do that? I think one answer to that question, if
I have learned anything from working on Williams, will depend on
the specific contours as well as the underlying myth which spurred
someone on, and gave him or her a deep sense of self-definition.
I mean anything of course but the public mask, the face most people
see when they look at Hemingway or Hart Crane or Emily Dickinson
or Thoreau or Emerson or Poe. I mean that it is the biographer's
special agony and his or her glory to grasp *that* reality, that radiant
gist, that energy and direction, which should inform, *in*-form, a
thousand thousand otherwise disparate facts and make them dance
together. For without that inner understanding we see as in a glass

darkly, as in a winter snowstorm, the figures in the drama blurred, shadowy, halting, moving through a strangely cold and unrealized landscape. I think most successful biographers will tell you (or at least *could* tell you) that there was that moment of light when the inner life of their subject was suddenly revealed. At that point the earlier, partial images fell away and the inner consistency of their subject was impressed upon the biographer. What was many images suddenly coalesced into a unified figure, many-sided but nonetheless possessing a self, and then the dust particles—all those discrete facts—could be arranged into a major pattern. My experience has been that if this moment of light rings "true" to the biographer, then all subsequent finds will accommodate themselves to this pattern. If they do not, if the facts still insist on squiggling all over the surface, then the insight will have turned out to be partly light and partly an *ignis fatuus*, a shadow light beckoning into the swamps. Philip Horton, for example, published his biography of Hart Crane only three years after Crane's suicide, but he was not superseded by John Unterecker, whose life of Crane was published thirty-five years later in a study nearly three times as long. The reason this is so is that Horton managed to catch the truth of his subject and wrote passionately and to the point from that truth. In short, the pattern held.

Writing my own biography of Williams, I think the moment of realization came when I saw how central the myth of success through repeated failures had been for Williams. In teaching *In the American Grain*, for example, it became clear to me that Williams was dividing his protagonists into parts of a cubist mural composed in binary fashion of those who had "apparently" succeeded and those who had "apparently" failed. Among those who succeeded, Williams included Cortez and Jonathan Edwards and Ben Franklin, men whom Williams thought had failed to establish the intimacy necessary for genuine and lasting contact with their world. On the other hand there were such "failures" as Columbus and Montezuma, Père Sebastian Rasles and Daniel Boone, Aaron Burr and Poe. These figures were failures in the eyes of most Americans because they had not achieved the American Dream, ending their lives—all of them—disgraced, lonely, or misunderstood, though what they all had in common was their contact with the ground, a grounding necessarily figured for Williams in the woman, as much the necessary counterpart for him in his art as in his life.

It became clearer and clearer to me as I worked with Williams that he had pursued this theme through twenty years while he wrote his

Stecher trilogy and watched his family of immigrants (based as they were on his wife's family) become stranded on the desert shores of that same American Dream. I saw the theme again in Williams's dream of Washington, the father who had persisted in spite of repeated military failures on Long Island and Manhattan and up and down the New Jersey coast until doggedly he had won through and made his dream of America a reality, at least for a short while. I could see the theme at work again more subtly as a way of *in*-forming his epic, *Paterson*, where the poet's desperate search for a language with which to marry himself irrevocably to a place became his all-important work. By then Williams's sense of place had turned into a cry, the cry Williams swore Poe had heard when that poetic predecessor had gone in search of a country. So Williams heard his country crying out against him with all the anger and frustration of a Marcia Nardi, the very real woman whose very real letters he placed into the fabric of his poem by way of a judgment which he was willing by then to bring against himself for his own hubris in attempting to speak for the whole tribe (America) in the first place.

Williams's photographic negative of the American success story, then, became the generative myth, the underlying poetics, if you will, which in turn *in*-formed my own narrative of Williams. Early, Williams somehow became convinced that he was going to live a long and productive life. Somehow—perhaps because his grandmother had lived into her nineties and his mother lived to be a centenarian—Williams believed that the Fates would not cut his own life thread short, as they had cut short the life of Hart Crane. As a corollary to this faith, Williams also came to believe that he would have a very long and recurring creative springtime in which to get done what he knew he had it in him to do. In his early thirties he began to envision himself more and more as a revolutionary born into a time of revolutions: the revolution in American art signaled by John Reed and Big Bill Haywood and the Paterson strike of 1913, followed by Pancho Villa in Mexico and—most significantly—the Russian Revolution of 1917. Williams had only begun to come of age at that extraordinary period, and he knew he would need the next half century to work out the complex implications of his own revolution of the word. Incredibly, he nearly got the whole fifty years he'd bargained for, though it cost him more dearly than as a young dreamer he would have thought possible. And it is just there—in the crosscurrents Williams rode, the crest of the dream, the trough of rejection and misunderstanding—that my biography found its own mythic impulse. Here was Williams's version of the American success story experienced day by day in his own life drama.

Many critics and reviewers seem genuinely surprised that Williams could feel almost as if he'd been physically assaulted by the rejections and dismissals of Eliot, Frost, and the New Critics, as though the critics who killed Keats (in Shelley's mythopoetic version of the tale) had resurfaced long enough to bring Bill Williams down. That of course is nonsense, as it was nonsense in Keats's own case, where tuberculosis had a prior claim. But literary infighting, the politics of art, did have its grinding effect on Williams, as it had its effect on Eliot and Pound and Hart Crane and others. And even Gerard Manley Hopkins, who published virtually nothing in his lifetime, could feel a critic's barb by inference and smile sardonically to his friend Robert Bridges that, if such oblique references and dismissal constituted fame, he wanted no part of it. For Williams, however, the case was far more interesting and severe, for it was once easy in American literary circles to laugh Williams off. The *Partisan Review* did it, the Princeton circle did it, including Blackmur and Jarrell and others, *Poetry* did it, and by extension the entire British literary tradition did it. Everybody did it, or so it seemed. And though Williams could forgive, as he forgave the editors of the *Hudson Review* and sent them, in his last years, some of his best work, he could not always forget.

So, when Robert Lowell tried to patch things up between Williams and Eliot in 1948, Williams was willing to go along with the reconciliation (he did after all admire much the Possum had wrought), but he was quick to warn Lowell (and the rest of us) that the younger generations would be hard put to comprehend what Williams's literary skirmishes had cost his battered spirit. Did Williams actually remember Frost's snub at Bread Loaf, offered in the summer of 1941; did he remember it ten years later when he returned again to Bread Loaf? Yes, Williams did remember, as he remembered Eliot's dismissive conduct in 1924, and Duchamps's barb in 1916 and Jarrell's final downward reassessment of Williams when *Paterson 4* was published in 1951. Williams remembered because literature mattered so much to him. It really did matter how a poet put his or her language on the line. In the long empyrean view, as we turn the pages of our Nortons or other anthologies of American poetry and see Stevens and Williams and Pound and Eliot and Hart Crane enthroned side by side like larger-than-life Byzantine presences, none of this much matters. But in re-creating Williams's life, I learned early that all of this of course does matter. It mattered because there was a political and social judgment implicit in telling the world that a poem could be made of anything. I have said it many times, as Williams reiterated toward the end of his life. Anything is grist for the poem. Anything. Make it of this, of this, and this.

"Reading your biography," Williams's younger son, Paul, wrote me, "I can remember Dad's conversations over the dinner table. You brought them back to me. Apparently you were there too." For that is the job of the biographer: to re-create the inner drama of such literary skirmishes for those to whom literature meant life itself. Words, the words of the poem, the words of attack, the words of praise. All these words matter in the re-creation of a life. They matter as much as the victories and defeats of a Caesar, a Vercingetorix, a Nelson, a Pershing, a Patton, even though long after those battle sites have been emptied we may walk there in a tranquility which we throw backwards onto those earlier times . . . at our peril. What we want again in the literary biography is the hurl of voices shouting at or past each other, the words actually spoken in mid-passage and not the words remembered after the voyage is over. Discovery by "seaboard," Pound has it, not by Aquinas's map.

III

Literary lives, we should keep reminding ourselves, are after all made up of words. And if a biography is composed of words, we should look carefully at the ones we use. Is there, for example, a particular kind of language better suited to the telling of Subject X's life than Y's? Or at least a particular range of language choices? I think there is, *if* the biographer is able to possess himself or herself of that language. The language used to portray a figure like Henry James should be made to reflect the world of James, just as, in the vast verbal kaleidoscope of things, another language could be made to flesh the world of a Wallace Stevens and another the worlds of a Hemingway or an Emily Dickinson. Some will, I know, object to such an organic view of biographical language. Some may, for example, claim that such a suggestion smacks of what, in the days of neo-orthodoxy, was once called the mimetic fallacy: the attempt to imitate reality with language, or (in this case), the attempt to imitate the world of Subject X by seeing that world through the lens of Subject X's own language. Imagine doing Faulkner in the style of *As I Lay Dying*; or Joyce in the style of *Finnegans Wake*; or Emily Dickinson in the style of her own poems . . . or even of her letters. Other biographers will reject my suggestion because they do not have the ability to reconstruct either their subject's language or even the illusion of that language.

Of course such a direct imitation is not exactly what I have in mind either. What I mean is rather a simulation of the language of the subject whose life we are retelling. This is not to say the language which we hear in Williams's or Stevens's poems, or in the novels of Faulkner or Hemingway, but rather a simulation of a person's characteristic diction and syntax as we can discover those in letters, tapes, and memories of their speech: in short the language staple, the language as they themselves used it every day. To tell the story, that is, from the eye and mouth of Subject X, rather than from the outside, or at least to do this (more likely) as a strategy part of the time.

Let me give you an example of the kind of thing I mean. One critic took me to task for quoting some of the salty language and four-letter words which Williams finally managed to get into his written and spoken language. It apparently took Williams until he was in his thirties before he felt comfortable about doing this, having for so long been under his mother's injunction never to do or think a wrong thing. In allowing myself to reveal this "darker" side of Williams, this particular critic argued, I had revealed myself to be, like Williams, rather coarse-minded; by which he presumably meant using language unfit to be uttered in the presence of the truly great, such as Henry James and Proust and Dostoievsky, Mallarmé and Kafka. But it seems to me an easy enough trick for the critic to summon at least by name such an impressive pantheon, such a philosopher's circle, and yet never once raise himself above the humdrum quotidian of what passes for literary salon talk. There are very few of us indeed who have not at one point or another in our lives employed stereotypes in our language or found ourselves resorting to Chaucerian substandard English. Maybe it is because I am of a later generation, but if I had written the life of "Vinegar Joe" Stilwell I would not have agonized over Stilwell's characterization of polio-stricken FDR as "rubberlegs," as that fine biographer Barbara Tuchman says she did in writing *Stilwell and the American Experience in China* a dozen years ago.

It seems apparent to me at least that the biographer cannot afford *not* to reveal the darker shadows of his or her subject. For, like the novelist, the biographer must remain absolutely true to his or her subject. Biographers may well regret that their subjects used such language, just as they will probably regret the banal or vicious stereotyping of which their heroes were guilty (by which I mean comments about race, about religion, about sexual differences or preferences), but if it is part of the record, then certainly a representative portion of that material will have to be recorded or we falsify the story. The biographer must know not only what his or her subject said in the prepared speech before the podium in the glare of the public light, or reveal only the moments of lyrical perception and the splendid repartee; he or she must also show what the subject felt in the privacy of a letter or what was remembered off the record in conversation with a friend, an enemy, an outsider. Such glimpses will be rare enough anyway once the eulogizing and sculpting into marble begin. As a rule of thumb, therefore, the biographer would do well to learn from the linguist that all language—however highly charged—is acceptable if it helps to reveal the full dimensions of the subject, the chiaroscuro of light and dark which renders the portrait plausible.

Let me add, so that I am not misunderstood on this point, that I have little patience with those biographers who seem to be out to reveal the little or big secrets of their subjects for the pleasure of the scandal itself, without taking the necessary responsibility of placing those shortcomings in their correct perspective. There are biographers, regrettably, who show no real understanding of their subjects, who do not have the ability to show us the underlying strengths of a figure, and so set out to debunk (in a way Lytton Strachey himself never did) by holding up the shabby truths they have discovered like so much unwashed underwear. I find something disturbing, for example, about the treatment accorded Elvis Presley by his most recent biographer, Albert Goldman, not because he bares Presley's dark side, but because he seems to have gone to such disproportionate length to reveal what he learned from those figures, some of them mere hangers-on and some outrightly hostile to Presley, who surrounded the singer in his last depressed years. What this biographer fails to show us, meanwhile, is the very real hold Presley's music had on millions of Americans and others. We have the sordid facts of Presley's last years, the quantities of uppers and downers consumed, the casual sexual interludes, but where is the dream of the young singer before it soured, where is the truth of the legend which touched so many who make up the democratic ground of America? And why did that legend have the effect it did? It is not to be found, this other Presley, in Goldman's telling.

Norman Mailer, on the other hand, taking much less promising material in the life and death of convicted killer Gary Gilmore, did manage to explore the reality of the American West and to place the tragi-comic inversion of this world against the troubling and stark vision of early Mormons coming by wagon train to Utah. Mailer's is not, perhaps, a "true" biography since he is enough of an iconoclast to break generic bindings when he can, but for biographical texture his book by and large succeeds where Goldman's fails. This is because Mailer had the imagination to find a vehicle for Gilmore's felt sense of reality in the relentless, quotidian, and ultimately stark quality of the language he himself used, a language which employs the techniques of journalism in much the same spirit of Andy Warhol painting his meticulous reproductions of Campbell soups: a medium of flat, unadorned and even tacky sentences, precise as plastic rulers, the thin tissue of syntactical connectives simulating the thin tissue of unconnectedness which turns out to have been Gilmore's life. What strikes us too is that it is a life shared, except perhaps for its explicit violence, by millions of Americans. Goldman's language, on the other hand, strikes me as made up of a Madison Avenue confectionery of tinsel and plastic, half glitter and half function, much of it having the texture of that imitation marble where Presley's body lies, and serving much the same purpose of preserving a corpse.

What then of the cool, detached stance of the narrator as the model for the biographer, the speaker keeping an objective distance? Again, it is a matter of literary strategy, and I can see where an aloof, objective tone would do well for a life, say, of the historian Gibbon, or for a life of Baudelaire or Flaubert. But for the most part this sort of scientific detachment belongs rather in the case history or in those situations where the biographer needs to employ an ironic detachment to best engage the reader. This mode comes close to the finest reportorial prose, and might serve well in presenting a life of Nixon, say, or Kissinger. In most cases, however, where one is giving a life story, it should be the unfolding inner drama which asserts itself, whether that life is revealed in the poems and novels of a writer, or in the realized places of an explorer, a soldier, a statesman—in the operating room, over a Sunday dinner, on an assembly line, or on a lonely road lost somewhere at night. Let objectivity and distance be relegated to the preface of the biography or to the notes or the afterword or the index.

What we want after all in a biography is the subject alive and moving, and if this means evoking the Muse of the novelist as well as the more familiar Clio, that is all to the good. Let us see Hemingway driving his ambulance on the Italian front lines, or fishing for trout on Lake Michigan, or beginning to go to pieces in his mountain home in Ketchum, Idaho. Let us see Faulkner stopping to chat with friends on the town green in Oxford or drinking some of the local whiskey with the other hunters by a campfire at night, creating the Snopes clan half out of thin air, half out of the reality of the hill people. Let us see Dickinson stoop to stare quizzically at a bumblebee bumping about its work in the June sun there in the garden of her home in Amherst. Whitman tracking through the dirty snow of a cobblestoned alley in the Brooklyn of the late 1840s, his head filled with an aria he'd heard at the opera house across the river the night before. T. S. Eliot, tall and stoop-shouldered, in morning coat and frayed slacks, hair slicked and parted down the middle, a dog-eared copy of the Temple Classics translation of Dante's *Inferno* in his coat pocket, on a lunch break now from his wearying duties as clerk at Lloyd's, and staring down at the waters of the Thames, to recall that other great river with its brown gods, the Mississippi at St. Louis, along whose shores he had grown up. Let us see the mistakes and slights and economic worries, the estrangements and erotic engagements and the imaginative breakthroughs of these figures as and where they occurred, at eye level, and not through the clairvoyant eye of the omniscient and omnipresent narrator who, with deistic hindsight, looks out over it all and passes final judgment. We want the life, the life and not the marble tribute.

And yet we do want to see what these figures managed to achieve in their lives as well, for we have not chosen this man or that woman to blood with ten or a dozen years of our own life without hoping to have something in return. Writing a biography is, after all, rather like falling in love. At some point we must have seen something like a greatness in our subject, or if not that at least a uniqueness, demonic or otherwise, an achievement, or—if the life is minor—a special peculiarity in the life, a hunger at least for something, an ideal, however flawed, which draws the biographer on day after day. It was Geoffrey Wolff in his biography of Harry Crosby, that minor luminary of the American 1920s, who said that it was his subject's determination to transform himself through his own suicide into the Great Poet which held him riveted. Harry Crosby determined, Wolff tells us, "to translate himself from a Boston banker into a Great Poet by the agency of Genius," a genius "he calculated to attain by the agency of Madness." What is more, the final weird apotheosis of that madness would take the bizarre shape of Crosby's self-immolation. By keeping his word, Wolff argues, Crosby authenticated his life. "It is awful," Wolff tells us, "to watch someone with good eyesight and all his senses on full alert walk with gravity and determination toward the edge of a precipice, and keep going." Wolff disclaims any design on his readers; he is clearly not after a type or a lesson in the figure of this twenties American expatriate. Nor, he argues, is it the biographer's task to shape a subject's life to fit to a standard of morality or conduct, since the life, if sufficiently grasped, is always greater and more complex than any code or system superimposed upon it. And yet, we read lives because they do teach us something about human and moral conditions which none of us, I suspect, can ever escape or ever afford to dismiss. And they teach us even as they hold and fascinate us endlessly. A life unfolds, gathers to a greatness of momentum and complexity, and then inevitably begins to unwind, like those presences of Yeats's in the heavenly city of Byzantium, spinning in counterclockwise fashion, divesting themselves of the very lives into which they had spent the better part of their time on earth winding themselves in the first place. This process of self-realization unfolds about us and within us every day, occurring to a billion and a billion people. And yet. And yet what infinite variety within that basic arithmetical pattern we call life, we call death. Alpha and omega.

IV

Which leads me then to a word about the aesthetic strategy of endings and beginnings. Jay Martin began his life of Nathanael West with the moment of West's death. In a skillful narrative passage, Martin re-creates the scene: a California highway, summer, 1941. West and his wife, Eileen, slumped over in their new station wagon, West's body resting on the horn, still sounding, the car demolished, the two of them dead. Having killed off his subject, Martin explained a few years ago at an English Institute session on biography, he could get on with the business of recounting West's life as it would lead up to this irrevocable terminus. Like a butterfly collector, Jay Martin had his specimen pinned, with all its gorgeous colors on display. Justin Kaplan, in his biography of Whitman, appears to have employed a variant of this killing off of the subject by beginning his life of the poet in old age, waiting for the very thing he had all his life yearned after: sweet death and surcease. Only in the fourth chapter, then, do we see Whitman's own beginnings. By adopting this narrative strategy, it seems to me, Kaplan allowed us to see Whitman at the end of his biography not in death, but as an old man at Camden, walking through the tall meadow grasses and summer flowers along the peaceful river, himself at peace at last, like that other bearded patriarch, Monet, in his gardens at Giverny. But such a death-in-life scene as a strategy for Williams seemed particularly inappropriate, since death was the very thing Williams had struggled all his life against. Even Williams's still lifes, Jarrell has reminded us, swarm with a vigor which most poets never get into their presentations even of men and women. How much more so, then, in the life of the man himself.

I can tell you now that I had more trouble with the opening passages than I had with anything else in the writing of my biography. I wrote and rewrote those pages, trying to discover the most effective way to begin that book and introduce the reader to my version of Williams. I did not want to begin right off at the beginning. Rather, I wanted to present an image, a scene, which would catch something of the man's gestures and vitality but which would also signal something of the underlying drama of that life. For a long time my opening put young man Williams in an open boxcar with a group of other teenaged boys as the freight train ground slowly over the Hackensack River. In that scene Williams, sitting on the wooden floor, watches as one of the boys, a local kid from Rutherford with the marvelous real-life name of Dago Schenck, dives from the boxcar and down into the muddy river below. Such a scene, I had imagined, would have suggested Williams's own early passivity, his own delayed springtime—sexual, emotional, creative—as he bided for his own moment to make the great leap. It was a leap which came finally, in spite of his feelings of inadequacy and cowardice, only with the decision to begin *Paterson*, a decision which was not made until Williams approached his sixtieth year. This opening scene would have been the only partially fictive scene in the entire biography (at least to my knowledge), and by its placement as entrance song would have stood as an implicit statement to the effect that the biographer, if he is to make an artful biography, must use fictive devices so that the underlying truth of a person's life may be revealed. It would have said, essentially, that in writing biography what the biographer must finally deliver, in spite of all the research one can do, is not the life itself but a reconstruction, a simulation, a dramatization, an illusion.

In short, the biographer's reality is ultimately one more version of what Wallace Stevens meant by the Supreme Fiction.

Finally, however, I did not go with that opening, because my own thinking had shifted as I moved toward the completion of the biography. The original opening had stood as a metaphor, which is what I thought I had wanted in the first place: a scene which might reveal in microcosm the essential direction of a life. But that scene had been partially manufactured, as if to say: look, in spite of the years I've lived with Williams's spirit, I cannot give you the whole truth about him. And then it struck me. What hubris to suppose I or anyone ever could have done that. For to do that would have been to deny the central mystery of the human condition which no one—not Darwin or Jung or Freud or the biographer—can ever fully reveal.

Once I understood this truth along my pulse, I could try another entrance into my biography. It would be a much humbler moment this time, and yet one filled with significance, if only its metaphorical significance could be made to resonate. Such oblique metonymical strategies, a method of appearing to address a subject directly while revealing something other by implication, had been one of the lessons Williams as poet and as man had taught me. Approaching seventy and with most of *Paterson* behind him by then, Williams had finally gotten around to doing his public *Autobiography*. It is an effort filled with many good and true stories; indeed, it served as a primary source for my own biography, especially of Williams's earliest years. But it is a text filled too with significant omissions and distortions, and it was shaped according to its own *in-*forming myth, for Williams had meant to show the world how a small-town boy and provincial doctor had stayed at home while the others—like Pound and Eliot and McAlmon and H.D.—had gone running off to Europe. Williams's reward for staying at home had been to catch the prize, for by age seventy he knew he'd won through to being at least in some sense a representative American poet, a son in the venerable tradition of Emerson, Thoreau, and Whitman.

In the final scene of the *Autobiography*, Williams leads the reader back to the river, to the Great Falls at Paterson, this time in company with a friend and Williams's own grandson, Paul. It is early winter and there are ice formations everywhere about the park which sits above the Falls. Young Paul asks his grandfather to hurl one of those "ice cabbages," as he calls them, into the river below, and that act of hurling the object into the Passaic evokes in Williams's mind the image of Sam Patch, the local daredevil who had leapt from this very spot several times in the 1820s until he died, the clotted river finally killing him. Young Paul is of course both terrified and fascinated by the sheer magnitude of the spectacle, and yet he wonders out loud just how deep the river is at that point. So Williams ends his own life story here, at this place and at this moment, the present, with the son of his son calculating when and how he might ever duplicate Sam Patch's leap, the very leap Williams himself had finally willed himself into taking when he chose to begin writing *Paterson*.

It was with this scene, then, that I decided to begin my biography. In studying the original drafts for the *Autobiography* now at the Beinecke, I learned by chance that this visit to the Falls had taken place on New Year's Eve, 1950. The moment of Janus: the exact fulcrum on which the century itself rests. A looking forward and a looking back. By beginning just here, then, I would take Williams's own narrative closure and begin all over again for myself, telling Williams's story partially as Williams himself had seen it, but taking my own leap, as we all must, by restructuring Williams's rendering with my own. It would mean supplanting Williams's later version of the American success story as he'd presented it in the *Autobiography* with the deeper version which had guided him all those years while he had had to fight like a bantam to achieve a voice and have that voice heard. And of course, on the darker side, I would have to fill in the silences which Williams, with his wife Flossie looking over his shoulder, had chosen not to look at again in telling this official version of the story. And so I would begin by asking the same question which Williams had had his grandson—my own contemporary (and luckily my namesake) ask: Just how deep did the river (of Williams's life) really flow? What, in other words, had it really cost this American (one like me, of mixed ancestry) to dream of a language rising out of a particular ground, and to pursue that language and that dream daily for nearly eighty years?

The answers, such as they were, took over 800 pages of print, answers recapitulated for the reader once more in the biography's final pages. For the strategy of juxtapositions in that closure was meant to suggest that Williams's life, like the lives of his own heroes—Washington and Boone and Poe and even his own father-in-law—was both a vindication and a personal tragedy of a very real order. The singleminded pursuit of Williams's dream had cost him dearly in terms of his own life and the lives of those dear to him, especially his wife, whom he had loved in spite of self-preoccupations, infidelities, and the rest of it. I meant to suggest as much when

I showed Floss discovering her husband's small and wasted body turned toward the wall after the man had suffered one cerebral hemorrhage too many, and then juxtaposed that death with Floss's own death one May morning thirteen years later. Floss remains in part a silent presence throughout the biography because, after all, it is her husband who is taking center stage here. But this death was hers. And when we learn that at the end Floss made the decision to be cremated and her ashes scattered rather than rest beside her husband in death, it comes as something of a shock. I myself chose not to speculate on the reasons for that final decision, thus reminding the reader again that, in *any* life, no matter how long, much must remain, finally, a mystery. That having been understated, I could then get on with the business of the literary and imaginative significance of Williams's life, the legacy this flawed giant had left us, his sons and daughters.

V

Last, a word about the overall strategy of the biography. What I attempted there was something like a calculus of indeterminacy, a strategy of wresting success out of defeat. In my version of the metapoetics of the biography, I would inundate the reader with the river of facts surrounding Williams even as the reader should become aware that, if Williams's was a representative life, a life shared on many counts by many Americans in his roles of father, husband, lover, physician, citizen, and artist, it had somehow managed to move along another and unduplicated axis as well. In spite of failure after failure in that life, therefore, a crosscurrent paradoxically makes itself felt in the biography which, especially with the decision to finally do *Paterson*, resulted in Williams's breaking through and giving us a poetry commensurate with our particular sense of reality; that is, we, a people at cross-purposes with ourselves yet jostling in our pluralistic society in a kind of antagonistic cooperation.

On this level, the biography was an attempt to duplicate the central paradox of *Paterson*, which after all contains Williams's true autobiography, that poem which tells us finally that it is not any system of values that holds us together, whether we see those values as political, economic, or societal. Instead, what we get in *Paterson*—and what I tried to echo—is the sense of a life caught in the flux of reality itself, a life which, while in danger of being pulled under by the overwhelming flood of events, dares to question at every turn, responding to the flood of experience as well as it can at every moment. If it is *Paterson* then that contains the central Williams, it was my special task as biographer to respond as fully as I could to what that poem had to teach me as a life replica, my biographical form answering to Williams's more complex autobiographical one. "Weakness dogs him," Williams confesses toward the close of his epic,

> fulfillment only
> a dream or in a dream. No one mind
> can do it all, runs smooth
> in the effort, *tout dans l'effort.* . . .

It is the artist-father consoling the artist-son even in death. If I have told the life failingly, that too may be forgiven and may even be a virtue in the way we say that sweeping the dust together can be a virtue, apart from the elusive rainbow I earlier evoked. Williams for one knew that, being human, there could be no other way but to go haltingly when it is a man and not a god who is left to tell the story, to collect the dust and try to breathe life into it all again. *It is all in the effort.* . . . Let that be the biographer's as well as the poet's final defense. That and the intercession of the text itself, and the man or woman caught shimmering (perhaps) in all that dust.

Ten
Stephen B. Oates

Biography as High Adventure

*I found out that not only each book had to have a design
but the whole output or sum of an artist's work had to have
a design.*
William Faulkner

When I began graduate studies in history in 1958, I was fascinated by
the polygonal nature of the discipline. One could, I discovered, approach the past from any number of perspectives: as a social scientist
who studies forces and trends; as a quantifier who employs statistics
to illuminate patterns of behavior; as an intellectualist who explores
the role and impact of ideas; or as a humanist who focuses on the
human side of the past, examining how the interaction of people and
events shaped the course of history.

Almost from the start, I was drawn to the humanistic approach,
which made me something of a maverick even in graduate school.
For in the late 1950s, professional historians as a group were moving
away from humanistic history, and in the next thirty years would
function increasingly as sociologists and statisticians, pouring their
research into recondite, technical studies written largely for one
another. During those years, I traveled a different road from most of
my peers, a road that took me back to historical writing as literature—an old and honorable tradition too often disparaged in our
analytical time. Inevitably, biography appealed to me as the form in
which I wanted to write about the past, because the best biography—
pure biography—was a storytelling art that brought people alive
again, eliciting from the coldness of fact "the warmth of a life being
lived," as Paul Murray Kendall expressed it. As I studied biography
and historical narration, relishing the works of William Hickling
Prescott, Bruce Catton, and Arthur M. Schlesinger, Jr., of Paul

Horgan and Wallace Stegner, of Lytton Strachey and André Maurois, of Mari Sandoz and Marquis James, of Catherine Drinker Bowen and Kendall himself, I admired the way they transported me back into the past, giving me a sense of being there with the people they described. I also admired their literary techniques—their use of metaphor and time, their symphonic organization, their unabashed love for narration, and above all their conception and development of character. I reveled in the fact that artful biography was not abstract, was not an analysis of lifeless data and impersonal force, was not an academic lecture in which the biographer upstages his own subject, but was a form of literature like fiction. Unlike the novelist, the biographer is limited to what actually happened and cannot invent situations and make up dialogue. But like the novelist, the biographer must have an eye for detail and must learn the technique of controlled dramatic narration; he must keep his own voice out of the story so that the subject and his times can live again; and he must have insight into character, know how to depict complex interpersonal relationships, capture the inexplicable, and rely on the power of suggestion—especially through the telling quotation. At the same time, the biographer must have a professional mastery of the era in which his subject lived and died, which requires exhaustive, painstaking research in all the pertinent archival and printed sources. In sum, the pure biographer must be both a historian who is steeped in his material and an artist who wields a deft and vivid pen.

Because of my love for storytelling and literature, I found biography a tremendous challenge and eventually committed myself to the form, to trying to understand the past through the particular lives of individuals. In the process, I hoped to learn something about human nature itself and the universal truths held in common by people of all generations and all societies.

Over the next sixteen years, I conceived a biographical quartet on the Civil War era and its century-old legacies, a quartet that sought to humanize the monstrous moral paradox of slavery and racial oppression in a land based on the ideals of the Declaration of Independence. Four central figures made up my story—the slave rebel Nat Turner, the abolitionist and revolutionary John Brown, the Republican president Abraham Lincoln, and the civil-rights leader Martin Luther King, Jr. All four were driven, visionary men, all were caught up in the issues of slavery and race, and all devised their own solutions to those inflammable problems. And all perished, too, in the conflicts and hostilities that surrounded the quest for equality in their country.

Nat Turner, for his part, was the victim of human bondage, a brilliant and brooding slave preacher blocked from his potential by an impregnable wall. Nat's slave life was a prison of sorrow and frustration, a living jail in which he anguished over his condition and that of his people and longed for freedom all the more because he knew he could not have it. He was indeed like a powerful angel with his wings nailed to the ground. Only in his imagination was he free—free to live in the pages of the Old Testament, to identify with biblical prophets, to envision himself a singular man of destiny in the other world of his mind.

He suffered for another reason, too, for his wife and children were enslaved on another farm in backwater Southampton County, down in southeastern Virginia; he could do nothing to shield them from white people's caprice and cruelty. He was doomed to live apart from his family, an absentee husband and father who worked and slept alone on his master's farm.

At last, too intelligent and frustrated to remain somebody's property, aroused to a biblical fury by his own religious fantasies and the emotional revivalism of the time, Nat exploded at the system that oppressed him, inciting the most violent insurrection in southern history. Before it was over, it consumed more than 220 lives and sent Nat himself to the gallows at the age of thirty-one.

In *The Fires of Jubilee*, I tried to narrate Nat's story as graphically and accurately as I could. I wanted readers to suffer with him and see the world of slavery and the Old South through his eyes. That way they might gain melancholy insight into what it was like to be a slave. That way they might appreciate what Frederick Douglass said of slavery—that it brutalized everyone, black and white alike. Moreover, by placing Nat and his revolt in proper historical context, I hoped to convey how the insurrection rocked the South to its foundations and pointed the way to civil war thirty years later.

In contrast to Nat Turner, John Brown was a white northerner who hated slavery from the outside. He hated it because it violated God's commandments, because it contradicted the Declaration of Independence, because it was cruelly unjust to Negroes, because it threatened the nuclear family (he had read about the inhuman breakup of slave families), and because it imperiled him and his own family. Brown had striven hard to endure his trial on earth and to prepare himself for paradise and a union with his Calvinist God. Yet that same God, in a burst of omniscient rage, might well destroy Brown's "slave-cursed" land and sweep all Americans—Brown and his wife and children included—into the flames of an everlasting Hell.

As Brown smoldered over the manifold evils of slavery, he also suffered through a failure-scarred life that in itself reveals a great deal about human suffering. And it reveals much about nineteenth-century America, too, since Brown struggled for forty years to succeed in the system as a Christian businessman, only to fail again and again. Because it harbored slavery, Brown finally abandoned the American system and became a revolutionary like Nat Turner, convinced that God was calling him to a special destiny in Dixie. On a rainswept October night in 1859, he and a handful of followers—most of them young, five of them black—attacked Harpers Ferry in northern Virginia, intending to drive through the South and ignite a chain of Turner-style rebellions. Like Nat Turner, Brown was captured and hanged for his efforts. But he had repeatedly argued that, even if his raid should fail, it would cause a sectional blowup in which slavery itself would be destroyed.

He was prophetic. In southern eyes, he was Nat Turner reincarnated—a Yankee abolitionist sent by the "Black" Republican party to drown the South in rivers of blood. Because it linked southern fears of slave revolts with southern apprehensions about the Republican party, Brown's raid polarized the country as no other event had done, setting in motion a spiral of accusation and counteraccusation that bore the country irreversibly toward the Civil War.

By comparison to Brown and Turner, Abraham Lincoln abhorred violence and worked all his life inside the American system, a system he deeply cherished because it allowed men like him the right to rise—to better their station in life and harvest the fruits of their talent and toil. Yet Lincoln found himself trapped in a terrible dilemma. He personally hated slavery as much as Brown did and yet revered a political system that protected that very institution. He vacillated about when and how to resolve that dilemma, but after 1854 he never let his countrymen forget that slavery was a momentous *moral* problem that besmirched America's example before the world—and the judgments of history.

One of the supreme ironies of Lincoln's life—and of my quartet— was that he who spurned violence, he who placed his reverence for the system above his loathing of slavery, ended up smashing the institution in a violent civil war, a war that began because southerners equated Lincoln with John Brown and Nat Turner and seceded

128   from the very system that protected slavery from Lincoln's grasp. To save the American system, Lincoln rooted out slavery with the most revolutionary measure ever to come from an American president.

In granting freedom to the slaves, Lincoln also freed himself from his old dilemma. For his Emancipation Proclamation brought the private and the public Lincoln together: the public statesman could now obliterate what the private citizen had always detested. Then when both sides—the North and the South, Lincoln and the slave-owner—had paid for their complicity in the crime of human bondage, they could bind up their wounds and "do all which may achieve and cherish a just, and a lasting peace," as Lincoln proclaimed in his second inaugural. Some six weeks later, fuming at Lincoln for emancipating the "niggers" and blaming him for all the country's woes, John Wilkes Booth murdered the president at Ford's Theater, certain that assassination would make him a national hero. Out to a shocked and grieving nation went the news that Abraham Lincoln, sixteenth president of the United States, was dead in Washington, one of the final casualties of a war that had broken his heart and had now claimed his life, gone to join the other Union dead he himself had so immortalized.

Thus far in my story, all my figures in their separate ways had embraced violent solutions to slavery and racial oppression. Martin Luther King, by contrast, tried to combat such injustice through nonviolent resistance and the power of redemptive love. While he was as angry about the plight of black Americans as Brown and Turner, King learned from Gandhi how to channel his rage into a constructive and creative force for social change. Armed with the strength to love, he set out to break the chain of hatred in the world that only produced more hatred in an endless spiral. If the chain could be broken, he contended, then a new day could begin when all of God's children would live together in a symphony of brotherhood. By word and deed he aroused the black masses and stirred the American conscience more than any other leader in his generation. More than anyone else, he helped make Lincoln's Emancipation Proclamation a political and social fact. For the powerful civil-rights legislation generated by King and his nonviolent followers wiped out statutory racism in America, desegregating public accommodations and granting blacks the right to vote. The white president had issued the Emancipation Proclamation in the midst of the Civil War. Now, more than a century later, the black man and his people had made it stick.

Like Lincoln, King had an epochal sense of history and a world view of striking insight. He repeatedly stressed the need to understand that all life is interconnected, that all people are clothed in a single garment of destiny, and that "we aren't going to have peace on earth until we recognize this basic fact of the interrelated structure of reality." With that insight, King exhorted his country to abandon "the madness of militarism," to stop supporting repressive dictatorships in the Third World, to get on the right side of the liberating spirit of the age. With that insight, he called America to a great historical destiny: to demonstrate before the world that in this land of immigrants people of all racial, ethnic, and national backgrounds really could live in harmony and equality.

For twelve tumultuous years in the 1950s and 1960s, King marched and orated before a global audience, rallied the strength of his long-suffering people, and in the process won the Nobel Prize for Peace. At the same time he set an example of extraordinary courage—the courage to confront armed mobs with only the power of his spirit for protection, and the courage to confront the evil in oneself as well. In the end, King was assassinated in Memphis at the age of thirty-nine, a victim of the same conflict over racial tensions and national destiny that had claimed Lincoln's life in another April long before—and that had claimed the lives of Brown and Turner, too.

So my four biographies intersect on several levels—as the lives of their subjects intersected—and demonstrate how all were profoundly influential in the final destruction of American slavery and its legacies. At the same time, each biography can stand alone, for each is about a unique human being whose value, as Lytton Strachey would say, "is independent of any temporal process" and can be appreciated "for its own sake."

II

Because it must make the people of history live again, pure biography must be more than the compilation of research notes—more than the presentation of what one has gleaned from letters, interviews, journals, diaries, reminiscences, and other contemporary accounts. The prose of the biographer must radiate a sense of intimacy and familiarity, quite as though the author himself has lived the life and walked the ground. And this is a quality that can only be acquired by visiting the landmarks where one's subject lived and died. In the course of writing about John Brown, I journeyed across eastern Kansas where the civil war of 1856 had flamed, taking notes on the landscape, the murderous thunderstorms, and the howling winds that lashed the area where Brown's Station was located, and comparing these to descriptions recorded in Brown's time. As I stood rooted to the spot, the sounds of Bleeding Kansas—of artillery salvos, pounding hooves, shouts, and gunfire—echoed in the windy trees around me. And I could almost see Brown and his guerrilla band as they rode across the prairie to ransack proslavery homesteads and fight proslavery men. Later I visited the John Brown farm in the Adirondack Mountains of upstate New York. I stood at the front of Brown's cabin and stared at the frozen grandeur of the mountains, sensing the solitude as Brown sensed it. No wonder the old man felt at home in the Adirondacks. Up here in the mountains, as though suspended between heaven and earth, he could feel closer to his God.

In my search for Brown, I also visited Harpers Ferry, which is nestled in the Blue Ridge Mountains, at the confluence of the Shenandoah and Potomac rivers, and looks much as it did in Brown's time. With my notes and maps, I reenacted the entire raid, moving down from the Maryland mountains and descending on Harpers Ferry just as Brown and his men had done that rainy autumn night in 1859. I could almost hear the shouts and gunshots that rang over the town after Brown had captured the federal armory and arsenal, could see two of Brown's men getting cut down in a cross-fire in the Shenandoah, could see Brown himself fighting desperately to hold the fire-engine house from Robert E. Lee's federal troops.

Like my visit to Kansas and upstate New York, my journey to Harpers Ferry made Brown come alive for me. And in the act of writing *To Purge This Land With Blood,* I became utterly and completely immersed in his life and times. I dreamed about Brown and the Kansas civil war and Harpers Ferry, and once had a visitation from him, catching a glimpse of the old man in the doorway of my study, his steel-gray eyes fixed on me as I typed his story. Yes, he lived again in my mind, so much so that after the book was done and off in the mails, I lay around for days, lost in his world, beset with images of Harpers Ferry and Brown's trial and hanging.

The same thing happened with Nat Turner. During the summer of 1973, I went to Southampton County and retraced the entire rebellion, in what turned out to be one of the most memorable experiences of my life. In truth, being on the ground gave me a feel for Nat—a sense of the land he lived in, its forests, sounds, smells, and its people both black and white—I could have secured in no other way. Many of the homes that figured in the revolt still stood in 1973, haunted gray relics of time. I walked around in those cobwebbed dwellings, remembering where their inhabitants were when the slave insurgents attacked. As I stood in the weeds of one old manor, scanning the broken steps and the ruptured hallway, the unhinged doors and the sagging stairs inside, the place seemed inhabited, every room a museum of memories. And for a moment I could have sworn I smelled the aroma of freshly baked bread—and then the stench of manure from Nathaniel's stock pens. And then I could hear Nathaniel himself talking to his pregnant young wife in the kitchen there, could hear his nephews playing in the forest sanctuary in back of the house, could smell the acrid scent of cedar logs and see the slaves out in the fields beyond, singing those powerful spirituals that had moved me deeply to write about. And then—was that the sound of plunging hooves after all?—there was a frightful clamor in front of the house. And Will and Sam and the other horseback insurgents swept into the yard, leaped from their mounts, and broke into the house with axes; and I could hear the gunshots and the decapitated cries of dying people; I became one of Nathaniel's slaves who stood in inert terror in the shade of the barn, all the while Frederick Douglass's words echoed like thunder in my head (all are brutalized, all). . . .

When I wrote the Nat Turner book, I included an epilogue about my journey to Southampton County, trying to demonstrate that a good deal more goes into pure biography than reading documents and books in a library. Also, the epilogue had an artistic purpose, for I wanted to show that past and present really are a continuum. In fact, the last scene of the epilogue circled back thematically to 1832 and revealed a sad truth about the durability of human prejudice. In 1832, a Virginia newspaper editor, in defending gradual emancipation and colonization over immediate manumission, argued that whites could not overcome their racial hostilities overnight. In the epilogue, I quoted a Virginia banker who said the same thing in 1973.

As with John Brown, Nat Turner lingered on in my mind long after I had completed *The Fires of Jubilee,* as though his experiences—his life and death—were somehow my own. Unable to shake off thoughts of Nat, I sat one night in a dark and smoky lounge in Amherst, listening to a black musician play jazz on his trumpet and making all manner of connections with the slave music of Nat's world. Presently the musician launched into an old blues song, and

132   its mournful refrains transported me irretrievably back into Southampton County of 1831. With my eyes closed now and the trumpet
sounding sadly in the distance, I was with Nat as he ran desperately
through Southampton County, trying to elude the white patrols out
to get him with their dogs. I cried, "Run, Nat! For Christ's sake, run,"
as he crashed through the very forests and fields I had visited, until at
last he hid himself under a pile of fence rails. With dogs howling in
the distance, I stared at his face—a lined, contorted face, with shin-
ing black eyes—and was stunned by the depth of his suffering. Then
the scene changed, and Nat was struggling along the road to Jerusa-
lem, escorted by an armed guard through a sea of hostile whites. . . .
Then he was standing under the hanging tree, a chorus swelling
across the horizon as he prepared fiercely and silently to die. . . . And
for an eternal moment, as the trumpet wailed from across a universe
of time, I felt I wouldn't make it back from Nat's world, felt that I too
was doomed there, menaced by some unseen and unutterable violence about to descend on me like a guillotine. . . . But then I felt
a hand on my arm and opened my eyes in the gloomy Amherst
lounge. The trumpet player was sitting down at my table. Ah, Alden,
how good to see you. You play a mean trumpet, man. Meaner than
you know.

When I turned to Lincoln and set out in search of him, I ran into
difficulties. For one thing, his house in Springfield—an impressive
two-story structure that befitted his professional and social status—
is a popular historical site, clogged with sightseers come to pay
homage to the legend. I moved along in a bustling line of visitors, trying hard to envision Lincoln in his rocking chair there in the living
room, lost in one of his abstractions for which he became famous.
Once a spell even came over him while he pulled one of his boys in
a wagon. Lost in thought, he tugged the wagon over an uneven plank
sidewalk and the child fell off. But Lincoln was oblivious to the
fallen boy and went on with his head bent forward, hauling the
empty wagon around the neighborhood.

I left the house and went to his law office across from the state
capitol, where I imagined him sprawled across the old sofa with his
long legs stretched across two additional chairs. In this position he
read newspapers aloud, so as to bring two senses into play at once,
and prepared his law briefs. I also visited the Lincoln tomb, a re-
pelling shrine where a voice kept rasping over loudspeakers, "*Shh!
This is Lincoln's tomb. Shh!*"

It was almost as bad at the White House, which I visited at the time Watergate was getting into the headlines. Carried along by noisy crowds, I could only see a few of the rooms on the first floor. No chance to get a feel for Lincoln here.

But Ford's Theater was another matter. It has been so thoroughly restored that it looks now just as it did that Good Friday of 1865, when Lincoln came here for the last time. I sat down in one of the seats and gazed at the stage and the state box that overlooked it, trying to envision what it was like to be here on that grim and terrible night. Then across the street to the Petersen House and down to the dim little room where the doctors carried Lincoln after Booth had shot him. When I saw the four-poster bed where they lay Lincoln down, that night of nights came rushing forward—or I went hurtling back—and I could see the doctors laboring at Lincoln's side, could see Charles Sumner taking Lincoln's hand and bowing his head in tears, could hear Mary sobbing hysterically in the front parlor, while outside men and women, black people and white, waited in the rain as the president died. When I wrote *With Malice Toward None* and narrated the assassination, my visit to Ford's Theater and the Petersen House helped as much as all my research to make the final scenes live again.

I identified powerfully with the Lincoln of my story, for behind the myths, behind the god of marble and stone, I had discovered a man of rich humanity—a moral man who understood the complexities of human nature, a self-made man who was proud of his achievements, substantially wealthy, morbidly fascinated with madness, obsessed with death, troubled with bouts of melancholia, and gifted with a major talent for literary expression. I became so involved in his life that I got depressed when he did; I hurt when he hurt. When I left my study after a day's writing in his world, with brass bands playing Civil War music in my head, I was stunned to find myself in the twentieth century.

In pensive moments I still think back over his life, back over those tornado years of civil war, and I can still see him standing as he often did at a White House window, a haunted, harried man who did not know whether the conflict would ever end. Yet he fought it through to a total Union triumph, a triumph for popular government and a larger concept of the inalienable rights of man that now included the American Negro.

If anything, I identified even more with King, a man who lived in my own lifetime and whom I deeply admired (I had marched in the civil-rights movement in Austin, but had never met him). To gain a three-dimensional sense of my subject, I sequestered myself in the National Archives for part of one June, studying tapes, newsreels, and television recordings that featured King and his campaigns; reviewed Eli Landau's incomparable *King: A Filmed Record, Montgomery to Memphis;* and listened over and over to tapes of his speeches. Such records revealed telling details about King I might not have found in traditional written and printed documents: a certain gesture at the height of oratory, the tilt of his head in conversation, the way he said *"a-gain"* for again, the powerful sadness of his eyes.

But King lived most for me when I visited Selma, Alabama, to reconstruct the voting-rights drive he directed there in 1965—a campaign that resulted in the Voting Rights Act that enfranchised the southern Negro. In Selma, I met an articulate, animated black teacher whose home had often served as King's headquarters at the height of the marches. She led me into her den and pointed to "the very chair" (a family shrine now) where King had sat during all-night strategy sessions. She recalled how he was so busy, so much on the move in 1965, that he would often arrive at her home without a change of clothes and would have to wear her husband's suits, socks, and pajamas. She even showed me the bedroom where King slept. I could see him relaxing on the bed, cutting up with Ralph Abernathy and Andrew Young and telling his southern preacher jokes to the delight of his SCLC staffers. I could see him padding about in slippers and a robe and even going into the bathroom to shave. Because his whiskers were tough and ingrown, he could only remove them with an old-fashioned English straight razor and a special shaving powder that gave off a terrible odor. In 1965, his face looked tired and vulnerable somehow, but would light up in a boyish grin when he remembered something humorous.

My hostess also took me to all the sites of the Selma movement, wheeling her Gran Torino through town with uninhibited gusto. There was the green marble courthouse where the blacks had demonstrated for the right to vote according to the nonviolent principles King had instilled in them. There was the Edmund Pettus Bridge where Sheriff Jim Clark and his bullyboys had clubbed and whipped a column of marchers on "Bloody Sunday." And there was Brown Chapel, a quaint, red-brick building with twin steeples, where the blacks had held their mass meetings and launched their marches. As I stood in the church sanctuary, I could hear the sounds of those heady days: the clapping and singing ("Ain't gonna let nobody turn me around, Turn me around, Turn me around") and all the pep talks and orations of King's young lieutenants. The chapel was always packed during the mass meetings; people spilled into the aisles and through the doorways in back in order to see and hear "Dr. King." I could see him sitting in the pastor's chair in the glare of television cameras, his hands clasped in front of his chin and a pensive expression on his face, as he surveyed the swaying, clapping folk below. When he spoke at such meetings, he would plant his short legs firmly apart and move his fingers in little illustrative gestures to stress a point, and his incomparable voice would sweep the sanctuary: "Our cry to the state of Alabama is a simple one: *Give us the ballot!*"

The crowd: "Give us the ballot!" "Tell it, Doctor!"

King: "We're not on our knees begging for the ballot. *We are demanding the ballot!*" "Whatever it takes to get the right to vote in this state we're going to follow that course. . . . If it takes filling up the jails . . . if it takes marching on the state capital en masse and standing before the governor to demand our rights."

That of course is what they did, in what was surely the movement's finest hour. On March 21, 1965, some 3,200 zealous people left the sunlit chinaberry trees around Brown Chapel and followed King out Highway 80, popularly known as the Jefferson Davis highway, which led to Montgomery fifty miles to the east. Adhering to a plan worked out with federal authorities, three hundred Alabama Freedom Marchers went the entire distance, with United States flags whipping overhead and a Negro man from New York playing "Yankee Doodle" on a fife.

I retraced their historic march, taking notes on the scenery—the shipwreck Negro shanties with smoke curling from their chimneys, the snake-filled swamps and dense woods festooned with Spanish moss. I had fleeting images of King, now sharing a sandwich with a marcher during a roadside stop, now strolling at the head of the column, clad in a green shirt, blue cap, and sunglasses. And if I listened closely, I could hear voices and tramping feet rising on the wind.

> *Old Wallace, never can jail us all*
> *Old Wallace, segregation's bound to fall.*
>
> *Pick 'em up and put 'em down*
> *All the way Montgom'ry town.*

As the column moved through the rolling countryside, guarded by federal troops and lawmen, whites gathered at the roadside would yell and shake Confederate flags. At one point a sputtering little plane circled over the marchers and showered them with racist leaflets. They came from "the Confederate Air Force." As I reconstructed their journey on the Jefferson Davis highway, I kept thinking about the symbolic ties of the Civil War era and the civil-rights movement, about how Lincoln and King had fought for the same cause—for human uplift, racial justice, and national unity—against reactionary forces whose leading symbol was the Confederate flag. Yes, a hundred years later, King and his nonviolent warriors were still marching against that flag.

In Montgomery, the first capital and much trumpeted "cradle" of the Confederacy, the ranks of the Freedom Marchers swelled to 25,000 people—the largest civil-rights demonstration in southern history. By car and foot, I followed their line of march through the city, passed the Jefferson Davis Hotel and Confederate Square where Negroes had been auctioned off in slavery days. I was moving up Dexter Avenue now, jotting down my observations as people stared at me from cars and sidewalks. But I was all but oblivious to the Montgomery of 1977. In my imagination, I was part of that huge procession of 1965, with banners waving overhead and a Negro woman crying nearby, "This is the day! This is the day!" Like a conquering army, we surged up Dexter Avenue to the state capitol, where Confederate and Alabama flags were snapping over the dome. The spectacle was as ironic as it was unprecedented, for it was up Dexter Avenue that Jefferson Davis's first inaugural parade had moved, and it was in the portico of the capitol that Davis had taken his oath of office as president of the slave-based Confederacy. Now, in the spring of 1965, Alabama Negroes—most of them descendants of slaves— stood massed at the same statehouse, singing a new rendition of "We Shall Overcome," the anthem of the Negro movement. They sang, "Deep in my heart, I do believe, We have overcome—*today*."

Then, with state troopers and the statue of Davis himself looking on, King mounted the flatbed of a trailer, television cameras focusing in on his round, intense face. His vast audience listened, transfixed, as his words rolled over the loudspeaker in rhythmic, hypnotic cadences, older Negroes shouting "Speak! Speak!" "Yessir! Yessir!" "My people, my people listen!" King said. "The battle is in our hands. . . . We must come to see that the end we seek is a society at peace with itself, a society that can live with its conscience. That will be a day not of the white man, not of the black man. That will be the day of man as man. . . ." And that day was not long in coming, King said, and then he launched into the immortal refrains of "The Battle Hymn of the Republic," crying out, "*Our God is marching on! Glory, glory hallelujah! Glory, glory hallelujah! Glory, glory hallelujah!*"

As I stood before the statehouse, King's voice still seemed to echo in downtown Montgomery. Yes, his eyes really had seen the glory. And those who believed in him, who stood and marched with King toward freedom's land, became "a new Negro in a new South," as one told me, "a Negro who is no longer afraid."

On Highway 80, I saw another sign of the historic changes King and his people brought about in Dixie. I remembered how the Alabama state police had come to Selma at the height of the movement, rumbling into town in their menacing two-tone Fords, the stars and bars of the Confederacy emblazoned on their front bumpers. Twelve years later, I passed a similar state trooper car parked on the roadside. There was no emblem on its front bumper. The stars and bars of the Confederacy were gone.

It took me five years to complete *Let the Trumpet Sound*. During that time, I came to know King so intimately that I spoke to him in my dreams. I even fell into his speech rhythms when I talked about him in interviews and on the lecture circuit. Moreover, his teachings affected me personally, for I suffered a devastating tragedy in my life while I was writing his, and I almost succumbed to a paralyzing bitterness. But I learned from his example how to love again and "keep on keepin' on" despite my shattered dreams. In a strange and miraculous way, the very man I re-created became a warm, sympathetic friend.

When King died in my story, I was stricken with an overwhelming sense of loss, as though a member of my family had been killed. After I sent him home to Atlanta, to be buried near his Grandmother Williams whom he had loved so as a boy, I left my typewriter and staggered into my living room, unable to believe or to bear what had happened. And I cried.

For me, biography has not only been high literary and historical adventure, but deep personal experience as well. I have lived through four human lives besides my own, something that has enriched me beyond measure as a writer and a man. Most important, the experience of writing the quartet reenforced my lifelong conviction that the people of the past have never really died. For they enjoy a special immortality in biography, in our efforts to touch and understand them and so to help preserve the human continuum. Perhaps this is what Yeats meant when he said that "nothing exists but a stream of souls, that all knowledge is biography."

About the Biographers

Catherine Drinker Bowen produced a significant body of biographical work in her lifetime, including *Yankee from Olympus: Justice [Oliver Wendell] Holmes and His Family* (1944), *John Adams and the American Revolution* (1950), *The Lion and the Throne: The Life and Times of Sir Edward Coke* (1957), *Adventures of a Biographer* (1959), *Francis Bacon: The Temper of a Man* (1963), and *Biography: The Craft and the Calling* (1969). *The Lion and the Throne* won a National Book Award for nonfiction. Bowen was a fellow of the Royal Society of Literature and the American Philosophical Society.

Leon Edel, for many years Henry James Professor of English and American Letters at New York University and Citizens Professor of English at the University of Hawaii, is the author of *The Life of Henry James* (5 vols., 1953–72), *Bloomsbury: A House of Lions* (1979), and *Writing Lives: Principia Biographica* (1984). His life of James, which won a Pulitzer Prize, a National Book Award, and the Gold Medal for Biography from the American Academy-Institute of Arts and Letters, is now available in a one-volume edition. He is a fellow of both the American Academy of Arts and Sciences and the Royal Society of Literature, and an elected member of the Society of American Historians.

Justin Kaplan's *Mr. Clemens and Mark Twain, A Biography* (1966) won a National Book Award in Arts and Letters and the Pulitzer Prize for biography. He is also the author of *Lincoln Steffens, A Biography* (1974), *Mark Twain and His World* (1974), and *Walt Whitman, A Life* (1980), which won the American Book Award for biography. An elected member of the Society of American Historians and the American Academy of Arts and Sciences, he is currently writing a biography of Charlie Chaplin.

Paul Murray Kendall taught for thirty-three years at Ohio University, where he served as Regents Professor of English. In his lifetime, he produced a magnificent fifteenth-century biographical trilogy: *Richard the Third* (1956), *Warwick the Kingmaker* (1957), and

140   *Louis XI, the Universal Spider* (1971). *Richard the Third* was runner-up for a National Book Award and appeared in many languages, as did *Louis XI*. Kendall also wrote *The Yorkist Age* (1962) and edited *Richard the Third: The Great Debate* (1967). His *The Art of Biography*, first published in 1965 and nominated for a Pulitzer Prize, was reissued with a new introduction in 1985.

Paul Mariani, professor of English at the University of Massachusetts, Amherst, is the author of *William Carlos Williams: A New World Naked* (1981), which was nominated for an American Book Award for biography. He has also published three volumes of poetry, critical studies of Williams and Gerard Manley Hopkins, and *A Usable Past: Essays on Modern and Contemporary Poetry* (1984). He has taught in the Bread Loaf Summer School of English and the Bread Loaf Writers' Conference, and is co-editor (with Stephen B. Oates) of the Commonwealth Classics in Biography, a series published by the University of Massachusetts Press. Mariani is currently at work on a biography of John Berryman with the assistance of a Guggenheim Fellowship.

André Maurois, writer, public lecturer, and professor of French literature at Mills College and the University of Kansas City in the 1940s, was one of France's most prolific and distinguished biographers. His many "lives," which won numerous literary awards and appeared in many languages, include *Disraeli: A Picture of the Victorian Age* (1928), *Byron* (1930), *Lyautey* (1931), *Dickens* (1934), *Chateaubriand: Poet, Statesman, Lover* (1938), *Proust: Portrait of a Genius* (1950), *Ariel: The Life of Shelley* (1952), *Lelia: The Life of George Sand* (1953), *Olympio: The Life of Victor Hugo* (1956), *The Titans: The Extraordinary Lives of the Three Dumas* (1958), and *Prometheus: The Life of Balzac* (1965). Though he also produced an extraordinary number of novels, histories, and autobiographies, it was as a biographer that Maurois made his most significant contribution to literature.

Stephen B. Oates, Paul Murray Kendall Professor of Biography at the University of Massachusetts, Amherst, has published twelve books, the best-known of which form his Civil War Quartet: *To Purge This Land With Blood: A Biography of John Brown* (1970, 1984), *The Fires of Jubilee: Nat Turner's Fierce Rebellion* (1975), *With Malice Toward None: The Life of Abraham Lincoln* (1977), and *Let the*

Trumpet Sound: The Life of Martin Luther King, Jr. (1982). *With*
Malice Toward None and *Let the Trumpet Sound* both won a
Christopher Award for "affirming the highest values of the human
spirit, artistic and technical proficiency, and significant degree of
public acceptance," and both have appeared in several languages. *Let
the Trumpet Sound* also won the Robert F. Kennedy Memorial Book
Award. Oates's most recent book is *Abraham Lincoln: The Man
Behind the Myths* (1984). An elected member of the Society of American Historians, he is co-editor (with Paul Mariani) of the Commonwealth Classics in Biography, published by the University of Massachusetts Press. Oates is currently writing a biography of William
Faulkner.

Mark Schorer was a novelist, short-story writer, critic, and biographer who taught for some twenty years in the English Department of
the University of California, Berkeley. His most famous work was
Sinclair Lewis: An American Life (1961). In addition to novels and
short stories, he also published *William Blake: The Politics of Vision* (1946), *The World We Imagine: Selected Essays* (1968), and
D. H. Lawrence (1969). Schorer was an elected member of the
National Institute of Arts and Letters and the American Academy of
Arts and Sciences.

Barbara W. Tuchman, though disclaiming herself as a biographer, is
the author of *Stilwell and the American Experience in China,
1911–1945* (1971), which won the Pulitzer Prize for biography, and
several distinguished narrative histories containing biographical elements: *Bible and Sword* (1956), *The Zimmerman Telegram* (1958),
The Guns of August (1962), *The Proud Tower* (1966), *A Distant Mirror* (1978), and *The March of Folly* (1984). She also won a Pulitzer
Prize for *The Guns of August*, and in 1978 received the Gold Medal
for History from the American Academy-Institute of Arts and Letters, which the next year elected her president. She is also an elected
member of the Society of American Historians. Her *Practicing History: Selected Essays* appeared in 1981.

Frank Vandiver is the author of nine books, including *Ploughshares
into Swords: Josiah Gorgas and Confederate Ordnance* (1952),
Mighty Stonewall (1957), *Their Tattered Flags: The Epic of the Confederacy* (1970), and *Black Jack: The Life and Times of John J.
Pershing* (2 vols., 1977), which was a finalist for a National Book

142   Award. His "Biography as an Agent of Humanism" was the keynote address at a 1982 institute on biography, held near Austin, Texas, under the auspices of the Texas Committee for the Humanities. An elected member of the Society of American Historians, he is currently working on a biography of British Field Marshal Douglas Haig. Beyond his writings, Vandiver served Rice University as Harrison Masterson, Jr., Professor of History, acting president, provost, and vice president. In 1963–64, he was Harmsworth Professor of American History at Oxford University in England. He is now president of Texas A & M University.

Index